THREE CENTURIES OF LA RIOJA ALTA, S.A.

Nightfall at Áster (Ribera del Duero), with shades of blue as unforgettable as an evening walk among the vines.

Acknowledgements

This book is the fruit of the labours of several people who are all linked in some way to La Rioja Alta, S.A., to the extent that we consider them "family". Some of them deserve special thanks:

Julio Sáenz, our oenologist who, with the invaluable help of his wife Blanca, wrote the scientific sections, i.e. most of the book. He has managed to explain scientific terms with the elegance of a fine teacher.

James Bishop, Jimmy, for co-ordinating the production of the book and his tireless efforts in ensuring everything has gone to schedule.

John Hawes, for bringing his huge wealth of knowledge to the editing of this English edition.

Jesús Rocandio, a gifted photographer (and cook) who has been able to blend the art of "capturing the moment" with the science of technology and has succeeded in putting our feelings into pictures.

Xabier Rotaetxe, whose artistry has enabled him to produce drawings which, as well as being educational, elucidate the whole book and illustrate what photography is not able to capture.

We must not, however, forget our other collaborators. Gabriela Rezola, Samuel Fernández, Maria José López de Heredia, Rosa María Agudo and Ángel Barrasa, who read the book both out of interest and from a critical perspective, correcting grammar, vocabulary, cadence, style and technical information. And thank you to all our friends who allowed us to reproduce their photographs:

- Museo Vivanco de la Cultura del Vino: pages 38, 40, 44, 210 and 252.
- Fernando Díaz: pages 72-73.
- Laboratorios Lallemand Inc.: top of page 132.
- Pascal Chatonnet-Laboratoires Excell: page 134.
- Coopers Oak LLC: page 168.
- Victor y Amorim, S.L.: pages 198, 200, 202 and 204.
- Bodegas Vega-Sicilia, S.A.; Herederos del Marqués de Riscal, S.A.; Terras Gauda, S.A.; R. López de Heredia Viña Tondonia S.A.; Julián Chivite, S.A.; Codorníu, S.A. and Bodegas Muga, S.A. for the images on page 252.

First edition: July 2009.

Printed By: Industrias Gráficas Castuera.
ISBN: 978-84-613-0615-2.
Depósito Legal: NA-1012-2009.

Locations

La Rioja Alta, S.A.
Avenida de Vizcaya, 8. 26200 Haro. La Rioja.
SPAIN
www.riojalta.com / riojalta@riojalta.com

Torre de Oña, S.A.
Finca San Martín. 01307 Páganos - Laguardia
SPAIN
www.riojalta.com / baron@riojalta.com

Áster
Km. 55,1 Ctra. Aranda-Palencia.
Término El Caño. 09312 Anguix
SPAIN
www.riojalta.com / aster@riojalta.com

Lagar de Cervera
Bº Cruces. 36870 O'Rosal - Fornelos
SPAIN
www.riojalta.com / lagar@riojalta.com

THREE CENTURIES OF LA RIOJA ALTA, S.A.

Founded in the 19th Century,
growing in the 20th Century,
still passionate in the 21st Century.

DESCRIPCIÓN DE LA MARCA.

Consiste en una etiqueta en cuya parte superior central va la marca consistente en un paisaje en el centro del cual hay un rio sobre cuya superficie se leen las palabras »Rio Oja».

En la margen izquierda de dicho rio se ven tres arboles y un arbusto, y en la derecha un arbol, estando bordeada esta última margen por varias piedras, saliendo de la juntura de dos de ellas un arbusto que se inclina hacia el rio. Debajo de dicho paisaje se leen las palabras »Marca concedida».

A continuación está inscrito el nombre de la Sociedad con caracteres de letra redondilla francesa »La Rioja Alta», debajo del cual se lee »Sociedad de Cosecheros de vino», y en la parte inferior, a la derecha, la inscripción del pueblo donde radican las bodegas o sea »Haro».

Sirve para distinguir vinos.

Se empleará aplicandola por cualquier procedimiento a los envases de los mismos sin distinción de tamaños, tipos de letra y colores.

Madrid 30 de Diciembre de 1916.

DISEÑO DE LA MARCA.

MARCA CONCEDIDA

La Rioja Alta

SOCIEDAD DE COSECHEROS DE VINO

Haro

(Escala variable).

Madrid 30 de Diciembre de 1916.

E. MORALES FUENCARRAL 74 PRAL.DRCHA.MADRID
De la "Asociación Española de Agentes de Propiedad Industrial"

From the top of the Viña Cervera estate (47 ha) the vines resemble a carpet of leaves stretching from Santa Tecla along the Miño all the way to Portugal.

PREFACE

The members of the Board of Directors of La Rioja Alta, S.A. (R) and Torre de Oña, S.A. (T), from left to right and top to bottom: Jaime Gallego Agudo (Secretary), Fernando Maguregui Palomo (R), José Ignacio Sagarna Alberdi (T), Alfredo Ardanza Trevijano (T), Ángel Barrasa Sobrón (Managing Director), Maite de Aranzabal Agudo (R), Gorka de Aranzabal Urretabizkaia (R), Guillermo de Aranzabal Agudo (Chairman), Eduardo de Aranzabal Alberdi (R), Patxi de Aranzabal Alberdi (T), Gabriela Rezola Sansinenea (R) and Beatriz de Aranzabal Agudo (R).

One constant feature of La Rioja Alta, S.A. has been that we work with our friends and clients to expand our knowledge of the many factors which affect the production and ageing of wines. With this in mind, in 1979 we launched VENDIMIA (WINE HARVEST), a collectable series which later formed the basis of our book CIEN AÑOS DE RIOJA ALTA (ONE HUNDRED YEARS OF RIOJA ALTA), which was published in 1990 to commemorate the First Century of our bodega.

Since then almost 20 years have passed and we are into another century … there have been so many changes during that time, including in the world of wine. And, logically therefore, there have been many changes in our business. Today we have three affiliated bodegas which produce wines of great personalities, the LAGAR DE CERVERA (Rias Baixas), the BARÓN DE OÑA (Rioja Alavesa) and the ÁSTER (Ribera del Duero), and have more than 700 ha of wine in production in the best vine-growing areas, as well as bodega premises of which we are very proud… and much, much more which we wish to share with you.

And you, the enthusiast, have also changed – you expect more from us now. We must not "just" produce great wines but we also need to make our facilities available to you so that you can live the wine experience, not just drink the wine itself. This is wine tourism, which has had a huge influence on our Group. And there is so much to be said about new trends, technology, areas, styles, and varieties, among other things.

All of these changes meant that our book needed to be revised and this is the result. We have all personally put in a great deal of effort over the past year and have had an excellent team.

We hope that the true enthusiast will find in our book the most important details, ideas, techniques and all the poetry that can be found in a colour, a smell, a taste. We did not want to produce an encyclopaedic compendium, but rather an informative volume, to be dipped into, easily understood, accessible and creative, which the enthusiast will look at and read with passion and interest. We also hope to share the art and the science of wine as well as the unique features of the various wine growing areas where we have a presence (Rioja, Ribera del Duero and Rias Baixas), so that lovers of wine can count on a level of knowledge as a foundation on which they can then build with their own individual tastes and enthusiasms.

Manuel Ruiz Hernández and Sigfrido Koch, sadly departed but still much loved, wrote and chose the pictures for the first book. Following in their footsteps, our oenologist Julio Sáenz and the photographer Jesús Rocandio have done likewise with this new edition.

We hope that this work, full of science and love, will add something to wine culture and help you understood, learn about and love great wines and their world even more.

Guillermo de Aranzabal Agudo
Chairman

Cooks, rackers, stackers, workers from the vineyards, oenologists, administrative staff, salesmen, coopers, laboratory staff, security staff, PR staff – these are all part of the team which helps us to improve day by day. At the back is a portrait of our Chairman from 1973 to 2005, Guillermo de Aranzabal Alberdi.

Our lives are spent among the vineyards and fields, respecting the road already travelled and seeking new directions (the La Cuesta estate, 65 ha of Tempranillo in Cenicero).

OUR PAST, PRESENT AND FUTURE

NOTARÍA

DE

D. VICENTE GARCIA Y CALZADA,

CON RESIDENCIA EN HARO.

Copia de la escritura de *Constitucion*

DE

*la entidad civil denominada
"Sociedad vinicola de la Rioja Alta"*

OTORGADA POR

*Doña Saturnina Gª Cid, Dn Felipe Puig, Dn Dionisio
del Prado, Dn Alfredo Ardanza y Dn Mariano Lacort*

Á FAVOR DE

los mismos Señores

NÚMERO *202*

Autorizado el 10 de Julio de 1890

Imp. de B. González

Title page of the Deed of Constitution of the Bodega, dated 10th July 1890.

At the end of the nineteenth century, vineyards and indeed the entire European wine industry were devastated by an invasive plague: phylloxera. This tiny insect first appeared in Bordeaux in around 1870. French wine producers then began searching for alternative areas in which to cultivate their vines and soon arrived at La Rioja, which was still at that stage free of the dreaded plague. There they found a region with a thousand-year-old tradition of wine making but which had not yet adopted the modern techniques which would facilitate ageing and storage of their best wines over several years. The enthusiasm with which the native Rioja growers embraced the new technology led to frenetic activity and our local wine producers rapidly mastered the new techniques which the Bordeaux wine-makers had brought with them. These various upheavals led to the emergence of several new bodegas. One of these was LA RIOJA ALTA, S.A.

THE EARLY DAYS

On 10 July 1890, Don Daniel Alfredo Ardanza y Sánchez won over Doña Saturnina García Cid y Gárate, Don Dionisio del Prado y Lablanca, Don Felipe Puig de la Bellacasa y Herrán and Don Mariano Lacort Tapia and, in front of the Haro notary Don Vicente García y Calzada, these five signed the constitution of the SOCIEDAD VINÍCOLA DE LA RIOJA ALTA. The initial capital was 112,500 pesetas (€676), of which only 20% was spent. Those 22,500 pesetas (€135) started a passionate business adventure in which the five founders sought to realise the single dream of producing and ageing top quality wines.

The progressive philosophy of the founders is reflected in the choice of Doña Saturnina as our first President, a step which was rare at the time – and still is!

Nevertheless, the founding of our bodega was not the only important thing to happen in Haro in 1890. In that very year and ahead of anywhere else in Spain, electric lighting was installed in Haro and in Jerez, causing (along with other, less decorous reasons) local wags to coin the phrase "*Haro, Paris and London*" to describe the wonders of the world. This period also gave rise to an expression which we all use when nearing our home town: "*Look at Haro; just look at the lights*"

The bodega was situated in VICUANA, in the famous Barrio de la Estación de Haro, on estates owned by the Puig de la Bellacasa and Ardanza families, which leased them to the company. It was not until 1924

Our first oenologist M Vigier in 1890; he would barely recognise his bodega in its 21st century form.

that the bodega purchased in its own right the land on which its first winery stands. The much-vaunted, modern pro-European spirit was already alive and well in those early days, both in La Rioja and in our bodega. In just such a spirit a Frenchman, M Vigier, was hired as technical director and soon the predominant production method was that which we now call "classical". Our first three buildings are today offices, the cooperage and the Vigier cellar itself and, housed in a separate building, the fermentation plant in whose 33 large American oak vats we nurtured our grapes during our first 100 years. Those vats are still in use today, although not for fermentation.

A mere three months after it was set up, the company bought its first 3,500 Bordeaux barrels. It must be borne in mind that at that time wine was sold in its cask at prices which seem almost risible today: one 225 litre barrel of the 1890 vintage, i.e. both the wine and the barrel itself, would have cost 200 pesetas (€1.20). Furthermore, in that first year the grapes cost 1.375 pesetas per arroba (25 lbs), i.e. 0.13 pesetas per kilogram – the equivalent of buying 1,280 kilos of grapes for 1 euro! A year later, on 16 July 1891 the company became known as LA RIOJA ALTA and in 1941 it acquired its definitive name of LA RIOJA ALTA, S.A.

In 1892, when the bodega was still in its infancy, it was already producing 683,627 kg of grapes. Only a few years later, however, the vineyards were decimated by phylloxera and the enthusiastic wine makers suffered huge setbacks. Those were difficult years in which the entrepreneurial spirit of the wine producers was severely tested in trying to survive the huge crisis in the European wine industry. Considerable investment was needed to recover from the phylloxera plague, the majority of which was channelled into importing American root stock, which was immune to phylloxera. Native varieties such as Tempranillo could then be grafted on to this root stock. But no disaster lasts for ever and our founders emerged from the crisis more convinced than ever that they needed to focus on top quality wines. They decided to increase production of bottled wine.

The first reference we have to the price of wine by the bottle, which was sold to a household in Madrid, dates from 1902 when a bottle of the 1894 vintage (an 8-year old vintage!) cost 2 pesetas and a 1897 (a 5-year old vintage) 1.50 pesetas, i.e. about 1 euro cent. 26 February 1892 marked the debut of the trademark and symbol which is still in use today: the Rio Oja flowing swiftly between four oaks. It was first registered on 21 September 1908 by the Director General de Agricultura and renewed in 1916, as illustrated at the start of this book.

Very soon Europe and America began to appreciate the wines being produced by the company and during the following years in which shows and prizes were very much in vogue, the company won the following awards, amongst many others:

1893	Gold Medal at the Chicago Columbian Exposition.
1895	Silver Medal at the Bordeaux Universal Exposition.
1910	Grand Prix of Buenos Aires.
1911	Grand Prix of Toulouse.
1930	Gold Medal at the Ibero-American Exposition in Seville.
	Grand Prix at the Second International Congress of Vineyards and Wine at Barcelona.

Since then, the bodega's policy has been not to enter any tastings or competitions, although in some cases our importers and customers have entered our wines.

The world of wine is rich in tradition, classicism and respect for the past. This latter lives on today both in the manner in which the grapes are vinified and in the way in the wine is racked by candlelight. And it also lives on, of course, in the names we give our wines, many of which have their origins deep in our history.

In those early years, the only name under which the wine was marketed was that now known as GRAN RESERVA 890. For many years it was known as RESERVA 1890 to commemorate the year in which we were founded but the first digit had to be dropped for legal reasons, as was later the case with the RESERVA 904. It seems that, although it was not compulsory to put the year of production on the label, names such as these could leave a consumer confused about the vintage.

The first director of the bodega was one of the founders, Don Mariano Lacourt Tapia, who remained in this rôle until 1922 and in his first year received an honorarium of 5,000 pesetas (about €30).

DON MARIANO LACORT TAPIA, THE FIRST DIRECTOR OF THE BODEGA, WAS PAID 30 EUROS PER ANNUM

One of his first commercial challenges was likely to have been the question of how physically to export the wine to America. It must be remembered that at that time Spain had a very close relationship with the New World. Later came the Cuban War and, in 1898, the loss of the colonies.

The first harvests were carried out using mules. At that time the majority of wine was sold in casks, being bottled at destination by the customer, which is why the wine travelled in casks on those first shipments to America. Those oak-casked journeys were extraordinarily significant for La Rioja because they drew attention to the positive influence that the casks had on the quality of the wine. So it was that something as seemingly trivial as a storage container for shipping became a determining factor in the future of Rioja wines, influencing the ageing and the quality in a way which continues to this day.

Folklore has it that it was in those early years of the last century, when the vineyards were devastated by the phylloxera tragedy, that the term "Reserva" was coined. It is said that the French, because of the dearth of wine at the time, used to leave flagons of wine at the various establishments they frequented and on subsequent visits would ask for their "Reserve" wine. Whether apocryphal or not, the idea of a wine being kept aside specially, or "reserved", is what defines the Rioja Reservas today.

In 1904 Señor Alfredo Ardanza, a founder of LA RIOJA ALTA and also the owner of the Bodega Ardanza, proposed merging the two businesses, a proposal which met with unanimous agreement. To commemorate this event, which happened to coincide with one of the greatest vintages in the history of Haro, a very special wine, the RESERVA 1904, was marketed, a wine which today bears the name GRAN RESERVA 904 and is one of the most delicate and complex red wines in the entire Denominación de Origen.

Original 1890s cask, made of American oak, in which we fermented our first 106 harvests.

The growth of wine tourism and the food industry has necessitated major improvements to both the interiors and exteriors of all the bodegas.

These two Gran Reservas were initially presented in sealed bottles protected by straw packaging in wooden boxes. Some years later, we started to put wire onto the bottles, the logic being that the wire, like wax, was a protective seal which prevented someone falling prey to the dishonest temptation to switch the contents of a bottle with an inferior wine and then sell it on. The sealing wax was also a safeguard against cork disease. Subsequently and for many years the wire fulfilled an aesthetic role and was a link with the past. At the end of the 1990s we stopped using it after being advised by restaurant sommeliers that it complicated the opening of bottles.

But in those days everything was different – even the amount drunk. Tasio, our racking expert at the turn of the 20th century, used to say that he only drank four swigs a day. But, bear in mind that each swig was four mouthfuls and each mouthful was quarter a litre. That is four litres a day !

Racking was also different. The barrels were lifted by hand to form stacks, at the end of which landings were created, where the stacker was based. This activity continued, little by little, until five stacks were formed, at which point rollers were put into place along which the barrels were rolled to the end of the line and then lifted into position.

IT WAS THANKS TO PHYLLOXERA THAT THE TERM "RESERVA" WAS INTRODUCED TO THE WORLD OF WINE

It was a very difficult and physically demanding job, but for decades it was the only method used in La Rioja, until in the mid 1950s, Don Carmelo Hernando, invented a barrel lift, using a complicated system of counterweights. This was one of the first examples of "high technology" being used in the bodegas of Haro.

THE INTER-WAR PERIOD

From the end of the Great War until after the Spanish Civil War, the bodega enjoyed a period of calm during which there were no major changes.

In the years following the 1914 War, wine was transported by rail in large hogsheads to our agents, while a team of four or five people employed by the bodega (Pedro Palacios, Estefanía, "Piedra", etc.), went from agent to agent bottling the wine, sealing it, labelling it, etc. The bodega still has the special unlimited travel tickets that they used to travel as cheaply as possible. They spent many months away from home, travelling the length and breadth of the country. In 1922, after 32 years in his post, the director was succeeded by his son, Mariano J. Lacourt Tolosana, who filled the role for the next 16 years.

In the 1930s, the custom of despatching wine in bottles directly from the bodega began. However, even though the wine was now in bottle, it continued to be transported in casks, made in this instance of black poplar. The bottles of RESERVA 1890 were placed at the bottom, protected by yellow cellophane paper and straw packaging.

The black poplar casks, with a capacity of 100 bottles, were exported while the domestic market was supplied with bottles in the same straw packaging but in wooden boxes of 24 bottles. Later, the straw packaging was replaced with "carene" (papier mâché) bottle covers and then subsequently by pleated wrappings. Nowadays they are shipped in cardboard or wooden boxes with separators.

In 1935, when Don Luis Cabezón González was the director, the BIKAÑA brand was introduced; it is now produced exclusively for the hotel and restaurant trade in Haro, in recognition of and gratitude for all the support we have received from the city of Haro since 1890.

In 1936 the price of grapes was almost the same as in 1890, being some 0.18 pesetas/kg, but a year later the price had almost doubled, to 0.34 pesetas/kg (490 kilos per euro). It is logical to assume that this price increase was attributable to classic war-time inflation.

In 1940 Cuba was our most important market, importing predominantly VIÑA ARDANZA and a 3rd year wine, which was a forbearer of VIÑA ALBERDI. Export volumes continued to increase despite our import

agent's fear that *"with the 3rd year wine at 5 pesetas a bottle (3 euro cents) we will lose all our customers"*. Notwithstanding the price, sales continued to increase until, as one would imagine, the Cuban Revolution.

Meanwhile, we had established a very healthy market in Venezuela. RADIANTE, a semi-sweet white wine, was widely used there for celebrating Mass. This practice reached such a point that in order to export the wine we had to obtain, over and above the relevant analyses from the Oenological Centre in Haro, a certificate from the Bishopric acknowledging the suitability of the wine for Consecration.

On 28 September 1942, under the presidency of Don Leandro Ardanza Angulo (who had succeeded Doña Delores Paternina y García-Cid the previous year), a name was registered which, although it had already been on the market for many years, was to become the most famous and renowned name associated with the company – VIÑA ARDANZA. The name came from one of the families with the closest links with the bodega. Even today Don Alfredo Ardanza, a direct descendent of Don Daniel Alfredo Ardanza, a founder, is the director of our sister company, TORRE DE OÑA, S.A. And from the outset, VIÑA ARDANZA has, because

CASA FUNDADA EN 1890

MARCA   CONCEDIDA

La Rioja Alta

SOCIEDAD DE COSECHEROS DE VINO LIMITADA

BODEGAS EN HARO

DOMICILIO SOCIAL

SAN SEBASTIAN

MEDALLA DE ORO | MEDALLA DE PLATA
CHICAGO 1893 | BURDEOS 189

GRAN PREMIO
TOULOUSE 1911-BUENOS-AIRES 1910-1911

MEDALLA DE ORO
EXPOSICION IBERO AMERICANA 1900
SEVILLA

GRAN PREMIO 1930
EN EL II CONGRESO INTERNACIONAL DE
LA VIÑA Y EL VINO
DE BARCELONA

Sign outside our original head office in San Sebastian. In 1966 we moved the office to Haro, where it remains to this day.

of its inherent characteristics, its originality and its personality, been the jewel in our crown and the wine which most symbolises our bodega.

Throughout those decades the barrels were made entirely in our bodega by our team of five coopers. Thereafter, however, for many years our cooperage service made very few barrels, being mainly occupied with repairing existing barrels. In 1995 we started to make our own barrels again. Today we not only make almost all the American oak barrels used by the Group but we also import uncut wood from the United States and season it out of doors at the bodega in order to guarantee the final quality of the barrels.

RECENT DECADES

In the mid 1940s, the recently-appointed director, Don Nicolás Salterain Elgóibar undertook 13 separate business trips which resulted in him being able to report to the President, Don Nicolás Alberdi, the purchase of the Labastida bodega, in the La Horca district. We have stored and aged our Gran Reserva wines there, since 1977, in some 1,200 barrels and many thousands of bottles.

In 1946 the office was built as an extension to the first Haro premises and it still forms part of the present-day offices; a year later Don Nicolás Alberdi was named President.

Meanwhile, the directors continued to hold their regular board meetings, both at the Labastida bodega and the Haro bodega, at which some of them, such as Don Pedro, wrapped in his famous cape, and his brother Don Paco Ortiz de Zúñiga y López de Alda, would arrive in the elderly double-decker buses of the Compañía Alavesa. The latter, who became President in 1953, succeeded his father, Don Eduardo Ortiz de Zúñiga Montero, who was President in 1952.

UNTIL THE 1950s WE MADE OUR OWN BARRELS. IN 1995 WE RE-INTRODUCED THIS TRADITION AND BEGAN IMPORTING WOOD FROM THE AMERICAN FORESTS OF TENNESSEE, OHIO AND MISSOURI.

In 1952 the bodega bought its first bottling machine, which was also the first GIRONDINE (container transfer device) in La Rioja, with a capacity of 900-1,000 bottles an hour. This machine can now been seen in the gardens of the bodega. Until then the wine had been bottled and corked entirely by hand. Don Manuel Legorburu Bilbao later succeeded to the Presidency.

But times, and prices, change. In 1965 when Don Fernando Maguregui Ulargui (1963) was President, the 3RD YEAR wine was sold at 16 pesetas/bottle, the 6TH YEAR at 19 pesetas, VIÑA ARDANZA at 22 pesetas and the RESERVA 904 at 40 pesetas/bottle (24 euro cents).

In 1974 a new brand was introduced to the market, the VIÑA ARANA. It was not a new wine, but rather a new name for the classic 6 YEAR OLD vintage from the 1969 harvest. It is a fine, delicate, light wine with a subtle and intense bouquet. It took its name from the then Vice President, Don José María de Arana y Aizpurua, and was the perfect example of a wine which the Bordelais, who had worked in the bodegas of Haro, called RIOJA CLARET, so as to distinguish it from the so-called "red wines" normally produced from blending the sturdy wines from the Baja and Navarra banks of the Ebro river.

This wine was initially presented as a "Crianza" since traditionally in Rioja, wines were either denominated as being with or without ageing (i.e. "crianza") with the terms "Reserva" and "Gran Reserva" only being introduced later. Subsequently, later during the 1970s, VIÑA ARANA became a Reserva.

OUR GROUP EXPANDED GREATLY DURING THE 1970s AND 1980s

In 1970 new premises were built for the barrels. By 1987, we had recognised the huge improvement that stainless steel vats offered over oak barrels in the fermentation process (and only in the fermentation process), both in terms of hygiene and temperature control, and since then these premises have been used for fermentation in stainless steel vats. Later, in 1996, the building was converted into a bottling plant when our new fermentation premises at Labastida became operational.

In the 1970s the last two local offices of the bodega, in San Sebastián and Madrid, were closed. A period of rapid expansion began, with the bodega acquiring estates in Tudelilla (32 hectares), Montecillo (25 ha) and Rodezno (the Viña Arana estate, of 36 ha, and the Viña Alberdi estate, of 22 ha). All of these estates are now much larger.

The expansion of the bodega required fresh investment in barrels and in 1973 the land next to our original buildings was bought from Don Otto Horcher where, a year later, the dining facilities were opened, housed within the MARQUÉS DE HARO y VIÑA ALBERDI bodegas.

The VIÑA ALBERDI in fact replaced the previous 3 YEAR OLD vintage and owes its name to Don Nicolás Alberdi who, as mentioned earlier, was our President between 1947 and 1952. The name was registered in 1978, with the first vintage being the '74. It is the youngest style of wine that we currently offer and is the only Crianza we offer on the domestic market, although it is available for export as a Reserva.

In 1979 Don Fernando Maguregui Ulargui (President since 1973), a fine man and a first-rate administrator who, for health reasons, had been offering to stand down for some years, proposed Guillermo de Aranzabal Alberdi (grandson of President Don Nicolás Alberdi) as his successor. His resignation was accepted and the latter was named as his successor.

In the 1970s a major expansion of the bodega was begun and consolidated. The profits which we were reinvesting each year were not enough to finance these investments and we had to provide extra funding by way of several capital injections between 1973 and 1977, backed by large amounts of paid-up stock which reached almost 200 million pesetas (1.2 million euros). From 1978 to the present we have been able to fund development ourselves.

Metal poster with St. Mark's Square as the perfect backdrop for advertising our wines; it was used during the 1930s.

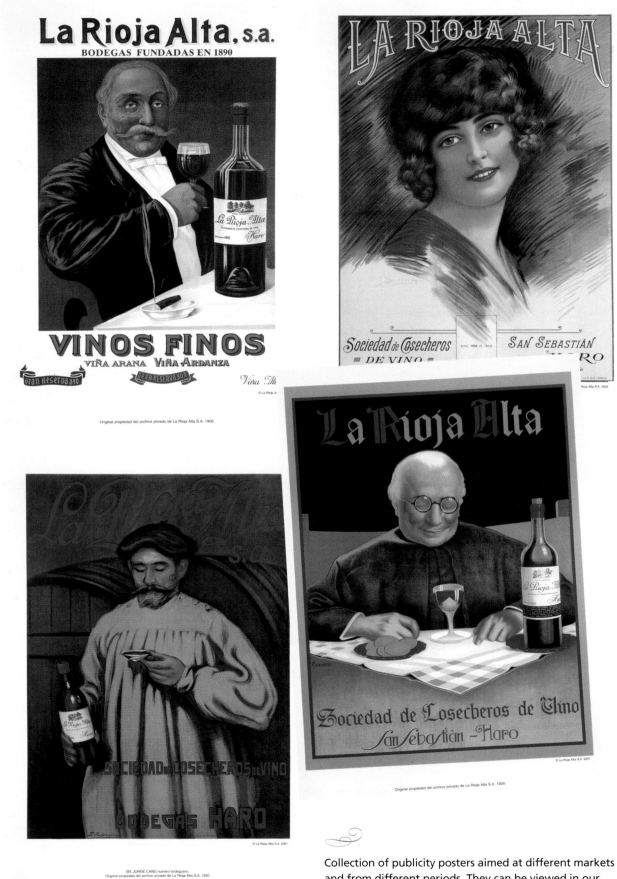

Collection of publicity posters aimed at different markets and from different periods. They can be viewed in our bodega.

In the 1980s we considerably expanded our buildings and vineyards and succeeded in completing possibly the bodega's most important task for many years, namely the defining of our products and clearly establishing the uniqueness of each of our wines. In contrast to the trend prevailing at the time, it was decided that we would increase the ageing of all our wines, both in barrel and in bottle. At the same time, we put great emphasis on the quality of the grapes coming into the bodega and on moving towards self-sufficiency in this vital harvest.

This uncompromising emphasis on quality required heavy investment from a medium-sized family bodega, but all the shareholders agreed with the policy and accepted the sacrifices that the investment would entail. So, in 1986, the racking tunnel and the VIÑA ARANA and the VIÑA ARDANZA premises were built and, following further expansion in 1990, they now hold a total of 20,600 Bordeaux barrels.

In order to further guarantee the quality of the grapes and our independence, we acquired the La Cuesta estate and renamed it "VIÑA ARDANZA". It is situated in the Cenicero region and comprises 90 hectares of Tempranillo.

IN 1987 WE SUPPLEMENTED THE OAK VATS USED IN FERMENTATION WITH STAINLESS STEEL VATS

In terms of defining the product, as mentioned above, there were also significant changes, both in terms of some brands being withdrawn and others being merged. One of these changes happened in 1980 when Fernando Fernández Cormenzana, who had a managerial role at the time, developed an excellent idea suggested by a shareholder, José Ramón de Aranzabal, and created the CLUB DE COSECHEROS DE LA RIOJA ALTA, S.A. with a small group of select clients. A 1976 vintage was selected and offered as a Crianza wine, albeit its quality gradually improved until it attained its current status as a Reserva.

In 1985 a brand was registered, the name of which will resonate over the coming years – MARQUÉS DE HARO. Then, in 1988, we launched VIÑA ARDANZA BLANCO DE RESERVA which perfectly accorded with our philosophy of making traditional Rioja wines, although this particular wine was only offered for a few years.

At the beginning of the 1990s production ceased of our remaining young wine (ROSADO VICUANA) and white wines (VIÑA ARANA BLANCO, VIÑA ARDANZA BLANCO DE RESERVA). We began to search outside the Rioja for an area to make a world-class white wine with a strong personality which would be clearly different to other Spanish wines. The result was that in 1988 we acquired and renovated a traditional bodega situated in the heart of Galicia, the LAGAR DE FORNELOS, S.A., which marketed the LAGAR DE CERVERA brand. The initial holding of 5 hectares has grown over the years to the present 75 hectares, growing nothing but Albariño, so as to ensure the best quality. The 1990s saw one of our bodega's busiest periods ever, both because of the favourable reception our products were given at home and abroad and because the bodega set its sights on wider horizons for the future.

In 1990 and 1991 the bodega acquired 75 hectares and planted them with Tinto Fino (also known as Tinto del País or Tempranillo); these are situated within the municipalities of La Horra and Anguiz, in the heart of the Ribera del Duero region, a denominated area which produces high quality wines. Later this holding was increased to 95 hectares and it and the magnificent bodega built on the site of the original farm now form the VIÑEDOS Y BODEGAS ÁSTER, S.L.

In 1994 the BOTELLERO DEL JARDÍN bottle store was built in Haro within the space of only 4 months. In order to do this, it was necessary to excavate the garden completely and the interior courtyard of the bodega, build the bottle store, and then re-cover it with earth and lawns. The new store can hold up to 2.5 million bottles.

On 27 January 1995 we took a 96.33% stake in TORRE DE OÑA, S.A., a beautiful bodega in Páganos-Laguardia which produces BARÓN DE OÑA, a Reserva red wine. This acquisition enabled us to become a producer of some of the finest wines in Rioja Alavesa. At the same time we have continued to expand the vineyard, buying another estate in the municipality of Cihuri (32 hectares).

On 15 January 1996 construction work began on the new Labastida bodega, which was built on our own land and is only 1.5 km from the bodega in Haro. The Labastida bodega was established under the name COMERCIALIZADORA LA RIOJA ALTA, S.L.U. and handles all fermentation and part of the ageing, both in barrels and in bottles. This has enabled us to improve quality considerably, particularly in the fermentation process, in part because of the state-of-the-art technology. We have also been able to increase our production levels to some extent and we now have greater flexibility when determining the ideal ageing periods for each brand and vintage.

At the start of the 21st century we are concentrating investment in the vineyard itself, planting 70 hectares in La Pedriza (Rioja Baja) with Garnacha, with the aim of guaranteeing supply of the top quality Garnacha grape which is very important for VIÑA ARDANZA. We have continued to expand the other estates in Rioja Alta, particularly in the municipalities of Rodezno and Briones among others. Today the group has more than 750 hectares of vines, spread across Rioja Alta (518 ha), Rioja Baja (70 ha), Rías Baixas (75 ha) and Ribera Del Duero (95 ha). We have also started to invest commercially, appointing an agent in Madrid and forging business links with agents in the domestic, American and European markets.

Our Chairman died in 2005 and was succeeded by Guillermo de Aranzabal Agudo, his son, who is the great-grandson of our former Chairman Don Nicolás Alberdi.

THE FUTURE

These have been some of the important dates in the history of LA RIOJA ALTA, S.A. Today in the bodega we still uphold those first principles laid down in 1890, zealously guarding the creative and entrepreneurial spirit of our founders. We have huge respect for our history and for the philosophy of our founders which can be seen not only in the way we make our wines but also in our brands, in our dealings with our customers and in our close relationship with the town of Haro.

Over the years, our Group has continued the tradition established by our founders of aiming for the very highest quality and is, as we have seen, expanding the premises and the vineyards, having at present a total of 45,000 American oak barrels for ageing, more than 8 million bottles of aged wine and more than 750 hectares in the best areas of Rioja, Ribera del Duero and Rías Baixas. Our current wine stocks equate to more than 8 years of sales.

To us, the most important thing is not the quantity of wine but its excellence. We want all our wines to be of a high standard and to achieve this we sacrifice large and easy sales.

We must continually strive to improve the quality of our wines as well as to adapt our wines to changing market demands and tastes but we must also make sure that we do not allow ourselves to be carried away by passing trends which can be so damaging in our industry.

We are also determined to meet our commitment to channel significant resources into meeting our social responsibilities. This is an area in which over recent years we have developed important projects relating, for example, to the improvement and the protection of the environment, working with various NGOs, improving the lives of immigrants and communicating the place wine has in our cultural heritage.

A corner of our new shop at La Rioja Alta, S.A.

Sustainable development is a priority for us and, to this end, our bodegas all have recycling and integral water purification systems which have enabled us to completely eradicate water wastage, including clean water. Likewise, we are developing Research and Development projects with the aim of limiting aggressive treatments in the vineyards as much as possible by using agricultural methods which respect the natural environment and using corks sourced from responsibly managed cork oak groves.

In 2007 we became the first bodega in Spain and one of very few companies in general to donate 0.7% of our net consolidated profits to working with non-governmental organisations to develop agricultural projects.

Furthermore, we have invested heavily in building several fully equipped, ecologically friendly hostels to house employees on site, the majority of whom are immigrant workers.

In 1998 we co-founded the Fundación para la Cultura del Vino (Foundation for Wine Culture), which is a non-profit organisation aimed at promoting the cultural values of wine and spreading greater knowledge about it.

We are committed to working in these and other areas, such as equal rights for women, working with charitable and cultural bodies, promoting initiatives which encourage innovation, creativity, quality, safety and training. In short, we understand that an active contribution to improving our society is also one of our obligations.

We hope that these little sketches and anecdotes will have given our readers a window into the life of our company and given them a better understanding of the aims which guide us.

"Bacchanel"
by Michel-Ange Houasse.
(born Paris 1680, died Arpajon 1730).
Oil on canvas, 125 x 180 cm.
Museo Nacional del Prado, Madrid.

A HISTORY
OF VINE
AND WINE

e will now set out a very brief history of the origins and evolution of the vine and wine through the centuries. Wine has always played a very important part in any civilization and culture, whether by way of its use in festivals and ceremonies or by its very prohibition, usually against the prevailing social mores. The viniculture revolution of recent decades has been profound, but if one thinks carefully about the way that wine is made today and the way in which it was made thousands of years ago, the differences are not in fact that great.

THE ORIGINS: FROM THE EAST TO GREECE

Recent studies have led us to think of Man and vine co-existing for thousands of years, since vines have existed since Man's earliest days. In the early days, the relationship was merely a question of eating the fruit of the plant; later, Man learnt to preserve the fruit as raisins and then, much later and possibly by accident, came the great discovery: wine.

The discovery of the remains of grape seeds in the Caucasian area of Chokn enabled the first cultivation of the vine to be dated to 6,000 BC. A millennium later, between the Tigris and Euphrates rivers where the civilization of Mesopotamia flourished, the first traces of tartaric acid were found in a vessel, although there was no direct evidence of vines being cultivated there. Different data show that wine was in fact being drunk in cities such as Babylon, Nipur, Ur and Endu; this was a drink that was produced in the mountainous regions of Syria and Armenia and journeyed to its final destinations in amphorae of fired clay, which could hold up to 10 litres.

Moving forward to 1,700 BC, we find a record of a deal between Bêtanu, a trader from Sippur, and Ahumi, requesting *"quality wine from the north, desirous of some 200 litres in the sum of 10 shekels (80 grams of silver)"*. According to this information, wine was a commodity which was 250 times more expensive than the same volume of grain.

From Mesopotamia and through the ports of Byblos, Tyre and Sidon, cultivation of the vine spread towards the Mediterranean, arriving in Egypt. The tombs of Abydos and Negada have yielded the oldest

Large pitcher showing a Dionysian banquet. Ceramic with red figures. Greek, 4th century BC; H 43 cm Ø 47 cm.
Camel loaded with amphorae. Ceramic. Nabataea, 6th century BC; H 19 cm, W 30 cm, Length 25 cm.
Both pieces are in the Museo Vivanco de la Cultura del Vino.

evidence from this time, dating to the third century BC, such as sepulchres and amphorae decorated with hieroglyphics showing activities related to vines, grapes and wine, as well as various references to the cultivation of vines and production of wine. We know, for example, that the harvest was carried out using a shaped blade whose morphology is almost identical to the so-called "corquete de Rioja" (a curved-bladed harvesting knife) and that the grapes from which the top quality must was obtained were trodden by slaves bound by ropes hung from the roof. In this regard a very interesting scientific study, "WINE IN ANCIENT EGYPT", presented at the British Museum in October 2005 and sponsored by the Fundación para la Cultura del Vino [Foundation for Wine Culture] (www.culturadelvino.org), proved that there was not only red wine but also white wine in the amphorae found in the tomb of the pharaoh Tutankhamen.

The Hebrews, enslaved by the Egyptians, also successfully cultivated vines and celebrated festivals with wine. Meanwhile in areas dominated by the Phoenicians there was considerable commercial activity which was critical in expanding vine cultivation towards the lands of Greece.

GREECE AND ROME

The Phoenicians introduced the art of viticulture into Greece, with the first references dating back to 2000 BC and relating to Dionysus, God of Wine. The Greeks developed techniques such as crop rotation, soil care and training of vines. Then came the first additives which were used as preservatives: salt water, turpentine, pitch and resin (the famous "retsina wines"). In ancient Greece wine was drunk in so-called symposia – "*To drink together*" – at which general, political and philosophical issues were debated passionately. The wine was mixed with water and the respective proportions depended on the importance of the occasion; the greater its importance, the less the amount of water. During this era the cultivation of vines spread across the Mediterranean basin and as far as Central Europe.

In about 460 BC Hippocrates emerged; he was the father of modern medicine and famed for his use of wine in many of his remedies against fevers and as an antiseptic. Meanwhile Homer described some of the wines produced in Northern Greece from a muscatel grape as being "as sweet as honey". Wine played a leading role at this time, alongside gourmandising and the pursuit of sexual pleasure, in festivals and orgies dedicated to the gods. In the ancient world, wine was synonymous with love and carnal pleasure but also with peace, relaxation, recreation and health.

Viticulture in Europe received a huge boost with the arrival of the Roman Empire, spreading to areas such as Alsace, Switzerland and the Palatinate, the banks of the Moselle, and England. In Hispania, the first traces of cultivation of vines have been established in Galicia, in the areas around the valley of the River Miño, and in La Rioja in Calagurris, (Calahorra) and Vareia (Logroño). The culture of vine growing enjoyed a period of great renown, begetting significant agricultural treatises such as those of Pliny the Elder or of Lucius Columella in which viticulture featured very heavily. The growth of "industrial" viticulture was marked, as can be seen from the recognition given to the products of different parts of the Roman Empire or from the celebrated maxim, "*Where vine growing withers, barbarism flourishes...*" and in the time

"The Sense of Taste". 1618 Jan Breugel The Elder (born Brussels 1568, died Antwerp 1625).
Oil on wooden panel, 65 x 108 cm. Museo Nacional del Prado.

"Bacchus with Cupid". Tapestry. Brussels, Belgium. Late 17th century. 173 x 219 cm
Museo Vivanco de la Cultura del Vino.

of the Emperor Justinius legislation was introduced to protect vineyards. So, for example, there was a law which threatened that *"any individual who is found guilty of cutting a vine stock, shall be subject to receiving lashes, removal of a hand or payment of double the amount of damage caused."*

The Romans were the masters of the Iberian wine growers. The first pressing, mixed with honey and then aged, was used to make "mulsum", which was served as an apéritif. The rest of the must was left to ferment in huge earthenware jars called "dolia" and was then clarified with ashes, clay, marble dust, resin, pitch and, like the Greeks, salt water. Once the wine had been put into amphorae, marked with the year of the harvest and the main characteristics, it was left to age in the upper rooms of the house, near the chimneys — in contrast to modern-day practices. The fall of the Roman Empire led to a significant backward step in viticulture due, in part, to the decline in the association between wine and festivities and the imminent and forceful emergence of the new Islamic Empire.

THE MIDDLE AGES

Following the fall of the Roman Empire, the task of developing viticulture and wine-making fell to Christian monks, who were committed to improving all aspects of wine production and who developed the vineyards left behind by the Romans. The arrival of Islam and the uprooting of vines in the lands it governed lead one to infer that vines were planted for the first time in northern, shady regions and, of course, in the climatic "corner" that is Rioja Alta. It can, therefore, be said that indirectly, Islam seen through the prism of modern wine-making, had a most favourable effect on vine growing. Clearly, this effect was not intentional. In both Rioja Alta and more northerly regions the vine took over *"ortos, hereditates, sernas"* and all types of worked land. This increase in vine cultivation was followed by attempts to force production through irrigation *"… ad rigandun ortos suos, aut vineas, aut hereditates"*.

The Arabs brought with them the Koranic prohibition on drinking wine. The Koran refers thus to the consumption of wine: *They ask you about wine and gambling. Say: "In them is great sin and some profit for men but the sin is greater than the profit."* (Sura II, 219) and later sets out an explicit and unreserved condemnation: *"O ye who believe ! Intoxicants and gambling and the altars of idols and the games of chance are abominations of Satan; eschew such abominations that you shall prosper. Satan wants to provoke animosity and hatred among you through wine and gambling and hinder you from the remembrance of Allah and from prayer. Will you not then abstain ?"* (Sura V, 90-91). The Iberian Peninsula was the scene of many battles between Christians and Arabs, with its unfortunate land being devastated by both sides. The terrible policy of "scorched earth" destroyed the crops and turned the region into a huge desert. The cultivation of vines was thus banished to the Benedictine, Cluniac and Cistercian monasteries in the Christian area. In some monasteries, such as at San Millán de la Cogolla in the Rioja region, there are still numerous references relating to the cultivation of vines in the Ebro valley, Sonsierra and the Rioja Alavesa.

The Reconquest enabled viticulture to become re-established, with absolute priority being the planting of vines. Religious communities and monasteries played a huge role in the replanting and the cultivation of vineyards. The celebration of the Eucharist in these communities depended on the fruit of the vines. For this reason, the first monks settled in the reconquered territories, establishing abbeys and monasteries and planting their vineyards as a top priority. Not satisfied with simply producing sacremental wines, the monks also provided various barrels for the abbatial and Episcopal bodegas. As a result, vineyards were established around monasteries and spread as far as the lands of the Duero and upper Ebro basins, the lands of Castile by the banks of the Eresma as well as Serena and the Tierra de Barros, adjoining the Moorish front. Elsewhere, the settlers arriving from the North replanted reconquered lands under the protection of the Military Orders of Calatrava, Santiago and St. John. As a result, vines were being cultivated in the 13th century throughout Iberia, except in the mountainous far north. Burgos became the wine trading centre of Ribera del Duero, Aranda and Peñafiel while the ports of Bilbao and Santander exported a wine from the Rioja region called "Ryvere" (from the Ebro river), which was particularly admired for its sweetness.

Mention must be made of how important the pilgrimages to Santiago de Compostella were at this time: they were acts of worship which changed the habits and customs of all the regions through which the pilgrims travelled. Hostels were built, as were hospitals, bridges, churches and monasteries, which were occupied by the Benedictines, Cluniacs and Cistercians, guardians of the secrets of cultivating vines and producing and storing wine. Along both banks of the Ebro river, numerous medieval wine producers set up, among which those at Laguardia, Briones and Haro stand out. In Galicia, where the influence of Islam was weaker because of its distance from Al-Andalus, it was possible to cultivate vines in the Miño and Rias Bajas regions. There is a legend dating from this time that the Albariño grape variety may have been Riesling, brought from the vineyards of the Rhine by Cluny monks on their pilgrimages to Santiago and initially planted in the Salnes valley and Cambados. On the other hand, the Galician version tells the opposite story, namely that the pilgrims took the Albariño grape to Central Europe and there, over time, it became what is now known as Riesling. What is not, however, in any doubt is that it was during this period that the treasurer of the Abbey at Hautvillier, Dom Perignon, accidentally discovered a way of producing a sparkling wine which was given the name of its region of provenance: Champagne.

FROM THE RENAISSANCE TO PASTEUR AND PHYLLOXERA

Following the reconquest of Granada and the discovery and subsequent conquest of the continent of America, cultivation of vines became geographically vastly more widespread. America was colonised from the north through Mexico, and in the south through Peru. Vine cultivation extended from Mexican soil right up to California, thanks to Franciscan friars who took vines with them on their evangelising missions. Some vineyards then took the name of the mission where they were established. It is also thanks to the Franciscans and the Jesuits that viticulture was exported from Peru onto Argentinean and Chilean soil.

The so-called Mediterranean model was the preferred one from the classical period up to the 18th century. The Greeks, Romans and, much later the English, preferred fortified sweet wines, made from white grapes. The northern European markets drank vast quantities of young wine, whites from the Rhine or red from Bordeaux (what the English call "claret"). Nevertheless they prized and paid more for the aromatic wines of Malvasia, from Cyprus, Greece, Malaga or the Canaries. At the end of the 17th century a fashion began for full-bodied wines such as Madeira, Port and Sherry which were either dry or sweet and had a relatively high alcohol content achieved by adding alcohol at the end of fermentation.

From the 17th century onwards, the significant growth in the population of Europe led to an increase in the demand for wine from the urban population, which continued until the beginning of the 18th century when the aristocracy, with its greater wealth, tried to create new, high quality wines as a symbol by which to distinguish themselves from the masses. Thus in England and ahead of many similar wines, the top quality red wines began to command a premium price; these were the wines which from 1855 became the Premier Grand Crûs of Bordeaux, promoted by Napoleon III. In 1707 Haut-Brion, Latour, Lafite and Margaux were already renowned in London. During this century we worked to establish Vizcaya as a centre for wine trading and Felipe IV granted the petition of Logroño vintners to be allowed to trade in the Vizcaya region. This made up for the arrival in Rioja of metal manufacturers and other products from the Vizcaya region. Logroño, along with Haro and Calahorra, was a trading centre for wine.

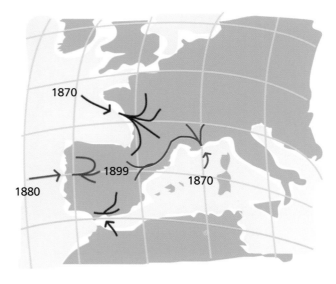

During the 18th and 19th centuries, the red wines of Bordeaux gradually dominated the Anglo-Saxon markets. Wine growing was established in South Africa around 1869, using European vine stock planted years earlier in the gardens of the Dutch East India Company, at the foot of Table Mountain, having been brought over on the Company's boats. Meanwhile in Australia, the first vines had arrived around 1790 at Parramatta and from these a commercial vineyard, funded by the state government, was planted to the north of Sydney, with later vineyards being established in the Melbourne area.

PASTEUR AND PHYLLOXERA

In March 1862, Emperor Louis Napoleon decided to summon France's leading scientist, Louis Pasteur, to the Tuileries Palace . The reason was to consult him about a serious problem affecting French wines which had already resulted in a large number of bottles, bought by reputable merchants and then sold to overseas clients, proving to be undrinkable. Pasteur's reputation was his discovery of alcoholic fermentation and how this was caused by the proliferation of micro-organisms. To find out why these wines were turning sour or becoming spoiled, he used a microscope to examine wines in good condition and samples of spoilt wine.

One of our first harvests, showing grape baskets, hopper and the reception and the destalking drum

A modern-day harvest in Áster, with manual selection table and strict hygiene control.

He was thus able to see that the samples of spoilt wine contained a huge number of micro-organisms (bacteria) which required oxygen to survive. When the samples were kept in airtight conditions, the wine was unchanged but when exposed to oxygen it spoiled. Pasteur discovered that the practical solution was to heat the wine, in its bottle, in a type of bain marie. This process later became known as pasteurisation. Pasteur also demonstrated that this practice could, moreover, be carried out without producing any deleterious effect on the wine. Unfortunately, the problems did not stop there. Some years later a far more devastating enemy appeared: phylloxera.

At the end of the 19th century serious diseases blighted French vines: oidium, phylloxera and mildew. Their appearance in France led Rioja, an area of Spanish red wines which had been virtually unknown until then, to adopt the French model, albeit with wines made from local grapes. At the same time as the Marqueses of Murrieta and Riscal were establishing their bodegas, Don Eloy de Lecanda, from Valladolid, began producing Vega Sicilia using, as did the Marques of Riscal, a combination of Spanish and Bordeaux grapes, among which Cabernet Sauvignon predominated.

Phylloxera was first discovered in 1863 in a nursery garden in a town near London and it appeared in around 1867 in French vineyards in the Gironde, Provence and the Languedoc. In Spain the press soon began to take an interest in this new plague and indeed in 1872 a ministerial edict was announced in relation to phylloxera. It was first detected in Spain 6 years later at the Lagar de la Indiana estate in Malaga. At virtually the same time it travelled south from France into northern Spain, invading the vineyards of Catalonia and spreading from there throughout the country. Rioja was invaded by phylloxera in 1899, with the first outbreak being found in a vineyard in Sajazarra, an area which despite all the publicity given to the subject remained completely unprotected. The following table sets out various dates highlighting the devastating effect in Rioja.

MUNICIPALITY	ANTICIPATED 1906 HARVEST (CÁNTARAS*)	AVERAGE HARVEST PRE 1900 (CÁNTARAS*)	% LOSS
Aldeanueva de Ebro	20,000	300,000	93%
Alfaro	20,000	250,000	92%
Arnedo	130,000	150,000	13%
Briñas	20,000	70,000	72%
Briones	70,000	350,000	80%
Cenicero	100,000	350,000	72%
Elciego	20,000	110,000	82%
Haro	35,000	240,000	85%
Lapuebla	28,000	100,000	72%
Oyón	8,000	80,000	90%
Páganos	1,000	20,000	95%
Rodezno	36,000	150,000	76%
Tudelilla	60,000	120,000	50%

* Cántaras = Container of c. 32 Pints

The only effective solution against phylloxera was, and still is, the replanting of vineyards with American vines or the grafting of European varieties onto American root stock. Other methods which have previously been tried include flooding, fire and various chemical treatments, all of which had limited success.

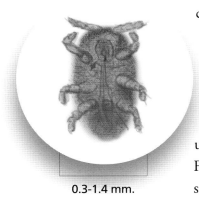

0.3-1.4 mm.

The phylloxera crisis had a huge social and economic impact and led to considerable social conflict. Between 1902 and 1904 there were up to 18 strikes by agricultural workers in the Haro area. The only solution for many people was to emigrate and abandon viticulture entirely. During the last 30 years of the 19th century, French wine producers and oenologists, whose vineyards had been decimated by phylloxera, began arriving in Rioja to buy wines and ship them back to their homeland so that they could sell them either unblended or blended with what little home-grown wine they still had. These French wine producers taught the Rioja producers the different techniques and scientific knowledge required to ensure that the wine survived from one year to the next and even improved during ageing. Some of these wine producers decided to settle in La Rioja which led, at the end of the 19th century, to some of Spain's most important bodegas being founded, many of which were situated near the train station in Haro, thus creating the Barrio de la Estación (Station Quarter), a name which is still used. As well as La Rioja Alta, S.A. (with its French oenologist M. Vigier), other bodegas which date from this period include CVNE, Bilbaínas, R. López de Heredia, Rioja Santiago and Gómez Cruzado. They were later joined by the Muga and Roda bodegas. These eight bodegas now form the renowned Barrio de la Estación in Haro.

THE 20TH AND 21ST CENTURIES

On 2nd April 1907 the Sindicato de Exportadores de Vinos de la Rioja (Rioja Wines Exporters' Syndicate) was formed. It was based in Haro and comprised 16 Rioja bodegas, 11 of which had estates in this area of Rioja. The Riojana, Bilbaínas, CVNE, Franco Españolas, Paternina, Azpilicueta, La Rioja Alta, S.A., Martínez Lacuesta and Carlos Serres bodegas all played important roles. The group was formed to guarantee the authenticity of the provenance of Rioja wines in overseas markets.

During the 20th century both production and marketing of wine undoubtedly underwent greater changes than in the whole of the previous four millennia and change is still continuing at an exponential rate. A process of change which had initially grown out of technological innovation has been further driven by the huge increase in communication media, tourism and the globalisation of markets.

In about 1910, the vineyards began to recover as a result of replanting with American root stocks, although this was the subject of much controversy. They were finally accepted and the biggest champions of this replanting approach were the "industrial" bodegas which began to emerge.

The 20th century witnessed an important change in agricultural methods, such as the introduction of mechanisation which arrived in viticulture later than other areas of agriculture, methods of working the soil and the introduction of chemical products, which brought considerable benefits and led to improvements in the quality and quantity of the harvests.

In the 1960s there was a significant technological innovation in Californian wineries: the use of stainless steel enabled fine wines to be produced for the first time in hot climates. There were significant changes to all the relevant processes including vinification, ageing, storage, bottling, transportation and the preservation of wines. Prominent among these were new oak barrels, cooling, installation of air conditioning and other improvements in the bodegas, the use of inert gases and of antioxidant additives, etc. In the 1980s Australians transformed both their viticulture and oenology, relying on both scientific research and technological advances. The Australians were not, however, satisfied with just their own domestic consumption and, aided by innovative marketing, made considerable inroads into the American markets and some of the markets of "Old Europe", predominately the United Kingdom.

The 1990s saw the arrival of new producers who had adopted the Australian strategies, namely New Zealand, Chile, South Africa and Argentina. Between 1990 and 2003 there were further technical developments which are likely to be long-lasting, such as mechanised harvesting, which is possible with many transportation systems, mechanisation of many of the green period operations such as bud and leaf removal, mechanised planting, etc. Selected vines were used for new plantings. One unresolved issue is that of mechanised pruning. Some vineyards do use mechanical pruning but only in test conditions, not in the fields. Possible types of mechanisation include robotic pruning using a robot which would prune in horizontal channels, but this would not be practical due to the huge costs, and mechanical pruning, i.e. a "one size fits all" approach to pruning with a cutting bar set at a pre-determined height.

New legislation was brought in governing the production of wine grapes and the Denominación de Origen quality control system implemented throughout Europe as a way of guaranteeing the quality of both grapes and wine. The first such system was introduced in Portugal and it was introduced in La Rioja in 1924. The international wine trade is regulated by the Common Market Organisation for Wine.

It was not long before the consumer realised their purchasing power and began demanding better quality and information. Consumers do not just want to drink wine, they also want to live and feel the wine and its world, to get to know the bodegas, their owners, the oenologists, to move among the barrels and around the vineyards, to come to tastings at the bodegas, etc. This is wine tourism, a new way of enjoying the world of wine, which is going through huge changes at the start of the 21st century.

Föhn Effect in the sky above Laguardia. The Cantabrian Mountains force up the mass of air from the north, condensing the water vapour and causing orographic rains (the barrier effect). On the hillsides of Rioja Alavesa, the dry air descends rapidly, increasing the atmospheric pressure and the temperature.

QUALITY
FACTORS

Viña Arana

The human factor has been, is and always will be the key to successful viticulture.

e are going to examine some of the factors which affect the quality of wine. Some are constants, some inescapable (climate, soil, organic factors) and others influenced by the wine-grower (variety, grafting stock, density, plantation scheme). Other factors are cultural, such as the training system, pruning, labour, fertilisation, irrigation, green pruning, chemical treatments and the harvest. Different combinations of choices yield different wines.

THE CLIMATE

This is one of the most important factors affecting both the ability to produce wine and its quality. Vines need certain climatic conditions which are governed by temperature, availability of water and sunshine. It is a plant which is sensitive to heat and to the frosts of winter and spring which markedly affect its vegetative development and the maturation of the grapes. It is widely considered that vine cultivation requires mean annual temperatures not below 9°C and not above 40°C. This type of climate is found between the 30th and 50th parallels north and 30th and 40th parallels south.

TEMPERATURE has a decisive influence on maturation of grapes and the composition of must and wines. Generally, those wines with a higher alcohol content, lower acidity and greater varietal character are produced in those regions where the mean temperatures are higher whereas wines with a lower alcohol content and higher acidity are found in regions with lower temperatures. Temperature also has a bearing in terms of its rhythm. It is opportune that just as the grapes are maturing there is an appreciable difference between daytime and night-time temperatures; this favours slow maturation which leads to varietal bouquets which are more fruity and suitable for quality wines. With regards to cold temperatures, in this context frost does not mean temperatures below zero but rather those below four degrees which affect the vineyards during spring and autumn. These cold spells hinder the vegetation process of the vines, causing low quality and green harvests. Persistent frosts of below four degrees during May or June point to a low quality vintage. In Ribera del Duero, where temperature fluctuations are more extreme from winter to summer and day to night, the grapes tend to protect themselves by developing a thicker skin, giving wines of a richer colour.

Many young people enjoy working together during the harvest. This photograph was taken in the Viña Arana estate in Rodezno (Rioja Alta). ⌒ The start of summer produces intense greens which contrast with the blue of the sky at our O Rosal vineyards (Rías Baixas).

SUNSHINE is measured in hours of effective sun. To grow properly during the vegetative and maturation periods, the plant needs a minimum of 1,200 hours of effective sunshine per annum.

Other factors include AVAILABLITY OF WATER, which is determined by the rainfall in the area and any irrigation system which may be in place. Traditionally, the vine has been considered a dry cultivation, being a plant which can grow in areas with low levels of water. Vines are thought to need an annual rainfall of some 350 to 600 litres, but this amount of water must be available to an adequate extent throughout the lifecycle of the plant. During spring there must, therefore, be sufficient water available to promote the plants' vegetative development whilst too much water during the flowering period is detrimental to the later fertilisation and pollination of the flowers.

VEGETATIVE PHASE	WATER REQUIREMENTS
Budding and bud break	13%
Vegetative growth	33%
Flowering and pollination	14%
Development of berries	10%
Veraison	17%
Berry maturation	13%

During maturation of the grape a minimum amount of water is needed to ensure that the leaves are healthy and able to carry out their chlorophyllic function, i.e. accumulation of sugars in the berries. Lastly, too much rain leads to a risk of dangerous diseases attacking the vines, and of mildew and mold in the clusters. Should this happen, the quality and colour of the wine is poor.

The precipitation in Ribera del Duero is low to moderate (450-560 mm rain per annum) which, combined with the long and harsh summers and winters and with marked temperature fluctuations all year, suggests a Mediterranean climate.

In Rías Baixas, rainfall is heavy during the winter and spring months and much lighter during the summer months. In autumn, the areas of low pressure dominate once more and usher in another very rainy season which increases the risk of fungal attacks in the vineyards. This high level of water makes it advisable to plant the vines on hillsides so that the water runs down to the river and does not soak into the ground but, at the same time, a hillside planting scheme does require grasses to be planted so as to avoid the hillsides being eroded.

MAP OF RAINFALL IN SPAIN

> 1,600	
1,201-1,600	
901-1,200	
601-900	
401-600	
201-400	
65-200 mm/year	

These three factors combine to form two climate zones, which are separated by an imaginary line known as the Wagner line, which begins in Portugal, below Oporto, crosses the Duero valley, passes through Burgos, traverses Logroño towards the Pyrenees via the Basque country towards Cahors and passes through the Loire Valley up to Lyon and Lake Geneva. Above this line is the Atlantic zone, with its mild climate, four distinct seasons and plentiful rainfall throughout the year. It produces wines of low alcohol content and high acidity. They are fresh white and red wines which when young retain the bouquets of the grape variety. Below the line is the Mediterranean climate zone, with less rainfall and more hours of sunshine. The wines produced here have a higher alcohol content and lower acidity.

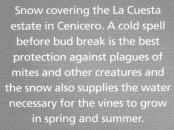

Snow covering the La Cuesta
estate in Cenicero. A cold spell
before bud break is the best
protection against plagues of
mites and other creatures and
the snow also supplies the water
necessary for the vines to grow
in spring and summer.

The bunches – plentiful, mature, healthy and bright, awaiting the harvest at Torre de Oña, S.A.

The climate of La Rioja can be described as "a shaft of Mediterranean light piercing the mists of the Cantabrian Sea". It is an area of very northern light within our peninsula. It also has another remarkable characteristic which is that the ocean winds cross the Basque country, i.e. the Cantabrian region with the lowest mountains, into our region much more easily than into other areas of the interior where the winds are blocked by the Picos de Europa or the Pyrenees.

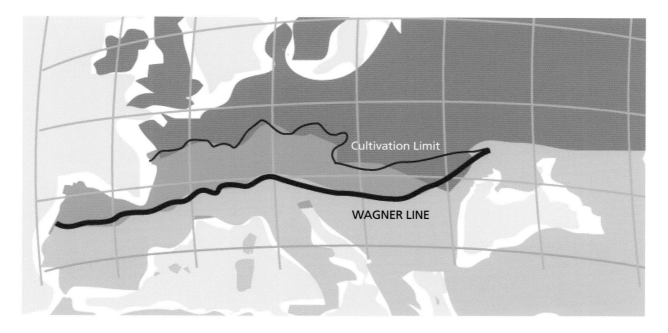

It is easy to imagine that those Atlantic winds blow into the vineyards a breath of quality, as these are the same winds that blow over Jerez, Oporto, Bordeaux, the Rhine, etc. In this regard, the vineyards of Rioja are at a serendipitous conjunction between Atlantic and Mediterranean climates. Within the region of Rioja itself the climate is very varied and a quick glance at the crops gives some idea of this, since between Haro and Alfaro there is terrace after terrace of vines and almond, olive and peach trees. The specific data for the areas where our bodegas are situated are set out below (averaged between 1997 and 2007):

LOCATION	ANNUAL RAINFALL	MEAN TEMP.	HOURS OF SUNSHINE
Haro (Rioja Alta)	490 mm	13.4°C	1,977
Logroño (Rioja)	439 mm	14.1°C	2,345
Alfaro (Rioja Baja)	348 mm	14.6°C	2,385
Roa de Duero (Ribera del Duero)	556 mm	11.3°C	2,260
O Rosal (Rías Baixas)	814 mm	15.2°C	2,068

Viticulture combines these data using the Winkler bioclimatic index which takes into account the active temperatures, i.e. those above 10°C, the days of light and the rainfall and refers them all to the 190 days between the annual bud break of the vine and the harvest.

Using this information, the "bioclimatic index" puts the Rioja Denominación in Zone 2 and Rías Baixas and Ribera del Duero in Zone 1.

A fine wine cannot, however, just be valued on the basis of its alcohol content alone, but also by its colour, taste and bouquet, which to some extent are at variance with the alcohol content. It is for this reason that fine wines bottled in Rioja usually have an alcohol content of between 12% and 13.5%.

It is important to understand that the wine of Rioja is a product which requires very particular climate conditions and the Rioja wine-producer faces, therefore, a constant risk of a poor harvest. Whilst Rioja wine is always of a certain quality, nevertheless it is not every year that the climate conditions allow a wine of such extraordinary or excellent quality that it is suitable to be a "Reserva", i.e. a wine capable of a long period of ageing.

THE SOIL

There are distinctions to be made between natural soil, agricultural soil and vine-growing soil. Natural soil results from natural changes that have taken place to the mother rock and are not a result of Man's intervention. Agricultural soil goes through the same changes and then through changes wrought by Man in the course of his agricultural activities. Vine-growing soil is created by changes to natural soil using techniques aimed at achieving optimum growth and a better quality of grape. The vine is a plant which adapts very easily to all types of soil although it prefers poor and rough soils.

There are various factors which determine the characteristics of a good vine-growing soil, which are explained on the following pages.

We collect the harvest in boxes of 20 kg to produce Lagar de Cervera (Rías Baixas), Baron de Oña (Rioja Alavesa) and Áster (Ribera del Duero).

THE DEPTH OF THE SOIL. This will determine the volume of earth across which the roots will spread to reach an area where better nutrients and access to water are found. In general, the best grapes come from soils which are shallow and poor.

THE TEXTURE OF THE SOIL. This determines the spatial development of the roots, the organ responsible for absorbing water and the nutrients necessary for a good crop, both in terms of quality and quantity. The different types of soil are defined by the percentage of gravel, clay and sand that they contain. A sandy soil is a loose soil which is poor at retaining water and nutrients and is very prone to droughts. A clay soil is very firm, more compacted, good at retaining water and nutrients and yields abundant crops. Loam soils are a mixture of the above two types and, like sandy soils, are the best for yielding quality crops and producing wines of great refinement, bouquet and fruitiness.

MINERAL ELEMENTS. These contribute to chemical fertility. The following are amongst the most important:

NITROGEN. This is the most important element as it is involved in the development and growth of the different organs of a plant. A lack of nitrogen causes reduced vigour and pale leaves and a consequential decrease in the crop. Excessive nitrogen causes accelerated vine growth, leading to poor fruit set.

PHOSPHORUS. This forms part of the vegetal tissue in a lower proportion than nitrogen. It promotes root development and is involved in the flowering phase and pollination. It is an element which has a positive effect on the quality of the grapes.

POTASSIUM. This is connected with maturation of the grapes, being an element which promotes sugar synthesis. Potassium deficiency causes poor fructification with few grapes, which are small and unripe. An excess of potassium leads to musts with low levels of acidity and very high alcohol content.

MAGNESIUM. This is a constituent element of chlorophyll which is essential for photosynthesis and, therefore, sugar synthesis. A deficiency leads to an overall weakening of the plant, with reduced root maturation, etc.

TRACE ELEMENTS. These include calcium, iron, sulphur, manganese, sodium, etc. They are found in smaller quantities and are involved in various metabolic processes in a plant.

ORGANIC MATERIAL. This comprises the residue of vegetal matter and animals which have lived in the soil and which have decomposed to form an amorphous colloidal mass, known as "humus", which is formed primarily of nitrogen, phosphorous, potassium and calcium. This natural humus has to be supplemented by organic material from fertilisers used by humans. In general, the vine requires relatively low levels of organic material to produce quality grapes. In fact, lands which are very rich in organic material and have high levels of water are those which are least able to produce quality wines, as they produce excessive vegetation and consequently poor fruit quality.

AVAILABILITY OF WATER. The water which is available to plants is capillary water and its supply depends on the texture of the soil. For a plant's organs to develop and grow, it needs an adequate supply of water from bud break right through to maturation of the berries. The plant's needs must be met from the water held in the soil and, if necessary, from irrigation. Insufficient water causes drought which in turn limits the development of the vine and this is an important consideration when choosing root stocks.

SALINITY. This is a factor which hinders vine development. High soil salinity causes drying of the plant to the point where it is no longer able to absorb water, even when it is available. Salinity resistance is a very important factor to be borne in mind when designing the plantation scheme for a vineyard and grafting stocks capable of resisting excess salt in the soil should be used.

THE SOILS OF RIOJA, RIBERA AND RÍAS BAIXAS

Vines are grown in different soils in Rioja. There are many different types of soils but the three most important are: chalky clay, ferrous clay and alluvial.

Following the River Ebro as it flows along "Las Conchas de Haro" and into the Rioja region allows one to see the vineyards on the left where the vines grow in ochre-yellow soils on terraces which descend from the Cantabrian Mountains down to the Ebro. This is Rioja Alavesa and the soil is chalky clay. On the opposite side are valleys and small rolling hills. The valleys are formed by the Oja, Najerilla, Iregua, Leza and Cidacos rivers. The vineyards are found on the plains by the banks of these rivers. The soil here is alluvial. The slopes bordering these plains are a distinctive red and are formed of ferrous clay soil.

The plant roots lead very different lives in these soils. In chalky clay soils (light sienna), after planting the vine puts out roots which gradually spread outwards and downwards. In ferrous clay soils (brown), once a plant has taken, its roots develop and penetrate slowly as it is growing on compacted, very clayey earth. There is, however, little possibility of the roots encountering rock.

Where vines are planted in alluvial soils such as those found in the plains along the river banks, their roots grow outwards and downwards through loose soils containing small, rounded pebbles. Having grown down about half a metre, the roots then, however, encounter a white crust, known as tophus, or tufa, which is pure limestone and which the roots cannot penetrate because of its hardness, the absence of any cracks and its releasing a substance, active limestone, which tends to dry out roots. The root is, therefore, unable to reach any great depth and is vulnerable to droughts and flooding. The use of tractors has, however, made it easier to break up this crust during planting with the result that the roots can carry on growing down indefinitely through layers of pebbles and gravels which alternate with sandstone.

The question arises as to which soils are the best for producing quality wines. There is no simple answer but it seems that the best soils are the chalky clay soils which cover almost all of the Rioja Alavesa and the municipalities of Fonzaleche, Sajazarra, Villalba, Briñas, Haro, Briones, Ollauri, Rodezno, Cenicero,

Clay soil.

Sandy soil.

Loam soil.

Traditionally in Galicia the harvest is brought in as "women's work", perhaps because they are more careful, sensitive and smaller than men, which made it easier when the canopied vines were low. A lady checking on the bunches of a Rioja vine just a few days before the harvest.

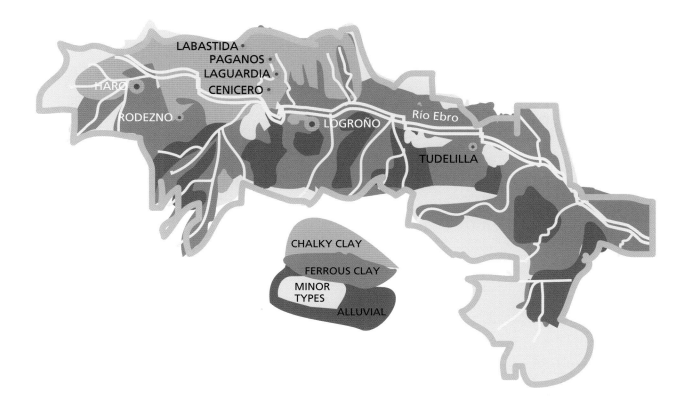

Fuenmayor, San Vicente, Abalos, San Asensio and Uruñuela across the wider Rioja region.

Nevertheless, there are vineyards on other soils which produce high quality wines, such as those of Tirgo, Cuzcurrita, Huércanos, Cordovín, Badarán, Ausejo and Tudelilla among many others.

The RIBERA DEL DUERO is located on the great northern plateau of the Iberian Peninsula, formed by an enormous, ancient basin and partly covered by Tertiary sediments. The soil comprises layers of sediments formed of silty or clayey sand alternating with layers of limestone and marl. A relief map of the region fluctuates between interfluvial hills, up to about 900 m high, and valleys with a topographical height of between 750 and 850 m.

The RÍAS BAIXAS Denominación de Origen is situated on a mixture of poor, acidic, sandy and thin soils at low altitude, generally below 300 m, close to the sea and at the lower stretches of the river courses.

THE HUMAN FACTOR

Just as the inventor of the wheel remains unknown, the moment when Man began to cultivate the vine might never be pinpointed. It is believed that vines were already part of nature, growing wild and uninhibited. Initially, Man did not cultivate varieties, being satisfied with collecting the wild fruits from

the vines. It was not until the Mediterranean civilisations were established that Man began to cultivate vines, control their development and produce better fruit. The Phoenicians, for example, did not settle along coasts but instead used navigable rivers to go deeper into the interior, as was the case in Ródano, until they arrived in Central and Northern France and Germany. They also travelled along the Duero and Tajo rivers until they arrived in Lusitania (Portugal), bringing stocks from other parts of the Mediterranean. In the case of the Rioja region, they travelled from the ancient Tarraco along the Iberus river (the present-day Ebro river) bringing vines imported from other parts of the world to towns such as Alfaro and Calagurris (modern-day Calahorra). Nevertheless, it was not until the Roman Legions arrived in Hispania that the high areas of the Rioja region were settled, establishing all the accumulated knowledge of Roman viticulture.

The arrival of Islam, resulting in uprooting in the conquered lands, may have led to the planting of vines for the first time in the shady northern regions and, of course, in the climatic "corner" of Rioja Alta.

Traditionally, the vine was cultivated in peripheral, poor and stony areas, with each variety adapting to

the climatic and soil conditions of the region. It is, however, worth pondering whether it was in fact the varieties themselves which selected the most suitable terrain. In any event, once Man mastered and understood cultivation of the vine, he began to use new techniques which enabled production of a higher quality and a greater yield. Man adapted the cultivation of vineyards to the peculiarities of his region, estate or "terroir", by using culture-specific practices (pruning, training of vegetation, fertilisers, etc.). A grower then concentrates on cultivating vines, adopting the terminology of a viticulturist, i.e. a person who specialises exclusively in vine cultivation. The viticulturist in turn specialises and acquires greater technical expertise, adopting new practices from emerging vine cultivating areas (Australia and New Zealand), adapting varieties from other vine-growing regions to his own natural resources and taking over lands which had previously not been given over to vine growing, rationalising his crops and mechanising the farm work (controlling diseases using chemical products, harvests in boxes, mechanical harvesters, pre-pruners) and introducing new training systems (trellises, canopies). In short, Man intervenes in his natural environment to produce wines which express the personality both of the land and of the viticulturist.

Julio Sáenz, our oenologist, and Pedro López Rollo, responsible for the estate, inspecting La Pedriza (70 ha) where we cultivate Garnacha, an important variety in the making of Viña Ardanza, being blended with Tempranillo.

ALTERNATIVE VITICULTURE

The current interest in the environment has led to new agricultural ideas, although some of them had already been implemented on a small scale since the beginning of the 20th century. Within this sphere of agriculture the most notable is ECOLOGICAL AGRICULTURE, which was first introduced in 1924 by the Austrian philosopher Rudolf Steiner. It is based on control of and respect for the environment, using organic fertilisers which have come from organic estates. Mineral fertilisers are seen as a supplement to such organic fertilisers, not as a substitute for them. Another important aspect is control of plagues and diseases by using cultivation techniques which mitigate the damage, which are economically sustainable and which do not affect the yield.

Biological disease controls are therefore favoured, such as the development of predators or parasites which are harmful to such plagues. Use of chemical products is tightly restricted to sulphur, Bordeaux mixture, silicates and very little else.

Another alternative is BIODYNAMISM, which is based on dynamic biology and on the power that is obtained from harnessing nature's forces. These techniques include the correct sequence of crops, the

alternatives being exploitation or renewal. It seeks to combine practical planting schemes, organic fertilisers of vegetal and animal matter, use of humus, use of sand in the soil, etc., as forms of pest control.

On the other hand, technical and technological changes have introduced new management systems which have been applied in agriculture. This is known as PRECISION AGRICULTURE, a concept of diagnosis and managing the vegetation in a crop, with the aim of improving productivity and quality whilst achieving costs savings and greater respect for the environment. It uses modern systems such as GPS Satellite Navigation to locate a vineyard in a specific position. Moreover, viticulture has reconsidered the suitability of information provided by satellite pictures (remote sensors) which, when taken with information provided for other variables, makes it possible to produce crop prediction models or feasible to make decisions about individual plots of land (zoning or differential management of cultivation). For example, as a result of the introduction and commercial use of crop sensors and monitoring systems of harvesters, it has been possible to see that there is wide variation in the quality of the grapes within the same plot of land.

This reflects difference in the soil, irrigation, need for fertiliser, etc., in different areas of the same plot of land which all need to be taken into account when it is being worked.

Traditionally Rioja was seen as a region producing coupage wines. This French term refers to the practice of blending wines from the same or different batch or harvest in order to combine their qualities. It is a practice which was adopted in Rioja after the phylloxera crisis, following the example of the great Bordeaux chateâux, with the aim of enabling Tempranillo to be stored and aged better. The Tempranillo of Rioja, with a very short and "early" cycle, posed huge maturation problems, particular in years of challenging weather. This led to a need to blend it with other varieties, such as Garnacha de Rioja Baja which brought the structure and alcohol needed to age the wine for long periods in barrels.

THE "TERROIR" CONCEPT ASSUMES THE PRODUCTION OF INDIVIDUAL AND UNIQUE WINES, ALWAYS FROM VERY SPECIAL VINEYARDS

The restructuring of vineyards during the 20th century was based on the random rearranging of the different varieties within a single plot of land, either due to ignorance of the variety being planted or because of a policy of trying to avert a new disaster in the vineyards.

Another factor to be considered was the practice of blending Tempranillo wines from different municipalities, places or vineyards with the wholesome aim of achieving greater uniformity and so reducing the influence of the harvest. This "coupage" model is the one which has always been used in La Rioja Alta, S.A., which produces wines based on blending different types of grapes from different plots of land.

More recently, in contrast to the coupage, or blending, technique, the concept of terroir has emerged; it is very widespread and used in the vineyards of Burgundy and was quickly adopted in Rioja Alavesa and Ribera del Duero. A vineyard is classified as terroir if it is a permanent entity in space and time, this entity being characterised by its homogeneity and the dominant and significant characteristics of its grapes, wines, type of soil and climate and the way in which they differentiate it from other vineyards in the surrounding area. The best example is in Burgundy, France, where the soils were first worked, used and studied by Cistercian monks before the end of the first millennium in the modern era. Having observed that conditions were better in some terroirs than in others, they then selected the best vines and improved their wine production techniques.

These typical terroir conditions were largely present in the vineyards of Torre de Oña, S.A., situated in Páganos-Laguardia, and in the vineyards of Áster in Ribera del Duero. The big disadvantage of the terroir concept is that it is very much governed by the climate, which can lead to the loss of harvests or of wines which do not reflect the idiosyncrasies of their plots of land. This was the case, among others, with the 2000 and 2003 harvests in Torre de Oña, S.A and the 2007 harvest in Áster, none of which produced any wine.

It was traditional to use the "coupage" technique with varieties from the same estate, interspersing red and white grape vines. This created beautiful fields with alternative rows of yellow, red, ochre and green leaves. Today the estates are planted with just one variety and "coupage" is done in the bodega.

Rogelio Rodríguez Giraldez, also known as "Castañal", is in charge of Viña Cervera and is seen here supervising the picking.

THE VINE

During flowering, the climbing vine protects the vineyard from the rain far better than a post and wire system. This is why it is used in Galicia, where the springs are wet.
The photograph shows Viña Cervera (47 ha of Albariño).

o be able to understand wine, its production and characteristics, particular attention must be paid to its raw material: the grape. This chapter will look at the physical components (bunches, clusters, berries, etc.) and the chemical components (sugars, acids, etc.). Lastly we will look briefly at the main varieties which we cultivate.

MORPHOLOGY OF THE VINE

The vine is a shrub made up of roots, trunk, vine shoots, leaves, flowers and fruit. It is an acrotomous plant, a liana which extends outwards until it meets a stake which it uses as a support to climb up. Pruning allows it to grow and be shaped in such a way that it can be cultivated.

After planting, the ROOT colonises the available soil during the first 5-7 years. During subsequent years, until the plant reaches an age of between 35 and 40 years it is nourished by the soil and it is during this same period that the plant undergoes its maximum development, both in terms of quantity and quality. After 40 to 50 years the quantity starts to decline although the quality remains steady or even improves. The root has various functions, the main ones being the absorption and conduction of water and mineral elements towards the aerial portion of the plant, the storing of reserves of substances which will enable formation of buds and growth the following year until the plant is able to photosynthesise materials for itself; the roots also fix the plant in the soil and produce hormones.

The aerial part of the stock consists of a twisted TRUNK formed of wood over a number of years, with an exfoliable bark, called the rhytidome. Its height depends on the training system and the pruning scheme. The trunk divides into BRANCHES, from which grow the STEMS and SPURS produced the previous year which, at the point where they fork out from the branches, form what is known as old wood. The BUDS are situated on the stems and spurs and will go on to produce the herbaceous shoots the following year. They are called spurs when there are two or fewer buds and stems when there are more than two.

Flowers appear on the vine in May or June; they are small, unostentatious and very difficult to see. The year's production depends on their being fertilised.

The SHOOTS (VINE SPURS AND CANES) are produced during the harvest year. They sprout from the buds which rest between the petiole and the shoot stem. These shoots will carry the leaves, the clusters of flowers which will later become berries and the tendrils. The vine tendrils are contained in the nodes which are swellings housing all the organs of the vine. The space between the nodes is called the internode and, except in certain anomalous situations caused by disease, they never house organs. There are different types of shoots:

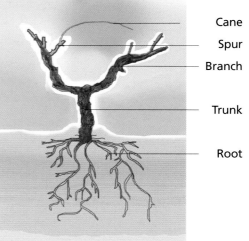

Cane
Spur
Branch

Trunk

Root

VINE SPURS/CANES: these are formed of two year old wood. These are the types of shoots which pruning aims to help, being the most fertile and responsible for the harvest. During the herbaceous period they are known as "vine tendrils" and as "canes" when they lignify and become woody, a process known as "withering".

SUCKER/TRUNK TRIMMING: this relates to material originating in old wood (trunk, branches). Trunk trimming or tidying refers to the removal of shoots when they are 10-15 cm long and it is carried out by hand during April or May.

LATERAL SHOOTS: The removal of lateral shoots is a green operation to remove those shoots which are infertile. It is carried out close to the flowering months.

The LEAVES are attached by the petiole in the nodes. The lamina is the most important part of the leaf, being responsible for photosynthesis, an essential process for forming the sugars necessary for the development of the plant and the maturation of the grape. Furthermore, it provides some of the characteristics which distinguish the different varieties.

The BUDS are formed by a sheath of scales and are covered inside with a whitish down. It is the organ which guarantees the plant's survival. The fertility of the buds is measured by the number of florescences per bud. In general there is a direct correlation between this number and the number of flowers. The quantity of buds and their fertility directly correlate to a stock's productivity, which is why in certain Denominaciones de Origen, such as the Rioja D.O.C., the number of buds which may be left after pruning is restricted.

Short pruning	12 buds/stock	6 spurs each with 2 buds
Mixed pruning	10 buds/stock	1 spur with 2 buds and a stem with 8 bud

In Garnacha, 14 buds/stock is permited because of its sensitivity to slipping (poor fertilisation).

The FLOWER of the vine is hermaphroditic, small, scarcely visible, green and white, with no bright colours, with very small sepals and a corolla with petals attached in the upper part. It is a pentamerous flower (5 petals, 5 sepals, 5 stamens). The flowers are grouped in florescences and, once fertilised, produce fruit which are berries or grape seeds. These are grouped in clusters which are formed of:

As the months pass, the green leaves of summer give way to a wonderful display of autumn reds.

STALK. This represents between 3% and 6% of the weight of the bunch, depending on the variety, the conditions during cultivation, pollination and growth period of the berry. The petiole is the small part of the stalk to which the seed of the grape is attached by a broadening, known as a "paintbrush".

THE BERRY. The fruits of the vine are produced through fertilisation of the pistil ova of the flower by grains of pollen. The berry comprises between 92% and 98% of the weight of the bunch and is formed by:

SKIN: This represents between 7% and 11% of the weight and is the external part of the berry. It is usually covered by a waxy protective layer, called "bloom", beneath which there are two layers of cells where the majority of the polyphenols (anthocyanins and tannins) and the aromatic substances contained within the grape are found. As well as the polyphenols, this part of the grape also contains the compounds responsible for varietal aromas in the layers closest to the pulp.

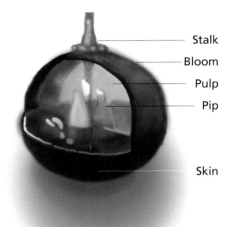

PIPS: These comprise between 2% and 6% of the weight of the grape berry and are responsible for reproducing the species; there are generally between 0 and 4. The most important of its compounds are tannins which migrate during maturation of the grape towards the skin, where they accumulate. Berry tannins are acidic and extremely astringent but, through polymerisation, they mellow and help to stabilise the colour.

PULP: This represents approximately 80% to 85% of the weight of the grape berry. It is responsible for collecting substances which have been synthesised elsewhere in the plant. It is principally made up of water and acts as the solvent for all the products which collect in it. Sugar concentrations later rise to between 150-250 g/l of must and can reach 290 g/l of must in over-ripe harvests.

Berries develop through various stages:

HERBACEOUS GROWTH. After pollination and during the first week there is rapid and intensive multiplying of cells leading to an increase in weight, which will determine the size of the fruit.

VERAISON. In our vineyards this occurs towards the middle of August. The chlorophyll in the berry disappears, it becomes softer to the touch and synthesis of polyphenolic compounds begins, causing red wine berries to turn a reddish colour and white wine berries to take on a translucent appearance and yellowish colour

MATURATION. This takes place between the middle of August and the end of September, following veraison. It causes important changes in the chemical composition of the berry, with the sugar concentration increasing and the levels of organic acids decreasing, turning an acidic and bitter taste to a sweeter and only slightly acidic taste, until the finished structure is achieved.

OVERRIPENING. The plant is still physiologically connected to the berry which gets smaller as a result of water loss through evaporation. There are some changes in the concentration of the compounds but such variations are of little importance.

83

The following are the most important compounds:

SUGARS: Quantitatively this is the compound which varies most. The basic sugars are glucose and fructose, which are formed through photosynthesis in the leaves and are stored in the pulp. All the factors which promote efficient photosynthesis also lead to increased sugar concentrations. The accumulation of sugars in the berry depends on the variety, the vine-growing practices and techniques used, the climate (the higher the temperatures, the greater the amounts of sugars), the soil (low levels of water and nitrogen, i.e. moderate fertility, increase accumulation of sugars), the foliate surface area (good exposure of leaves to the sun is important), the yield (kilos per vine or per hectare), etc.

ACIDS: The organic acids are the second most important chemical component in the bunch. The two main ones are tartaric acid and malic acid, with other acids (citric, succinic, etc.) being present to a lesser degree. The acids are stored in the vacuoles of the pulp and their levels generally fall during maturation. Malic acid is fundamentally free and its concentration depends on the cultivation conditions: the more vigorous the plant, the more effective the synthesis of malic acid. High temperatures lead to combustion of malic acid and thus to a reduction in the amount present. The concentration of malic acid varies greatly depending on the vineyard, climate, etc.

POLYPHENOLS: These are formed by tannins and flavones. Anthocyanins are responsible for the colour of red wines and are found solely in the skin, except in Tintorera varieties in which they are also found in the pulp. Tannins are the phenolic compounds responsible for the taste sensations of bitterness and astringency. They are found in the skin, the pips and the stalk. Formation of these compounds depends on the variety, the vine-growing practices used (foliate surface area and leaves well-exposed to sunlight, moderate load), the climate, (temperature during harvest below 15°C and significant difference between day and night time temperatures), the soil (low levels of water and nitrogen), etc. The peak

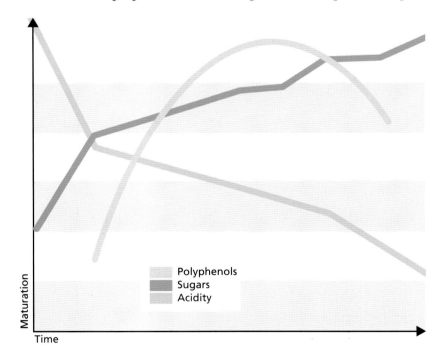

Polyphenols
Sugars
Acidity

Maturation

Time

accumulation of anthocyanins does not necessarily coincide with the optimum moment for harvesting if using pulp ripeness as the criterion. As a general rule, as maturation progresses there is an increase in sugars and a decrease in acidity. In contrast, polyphenol levels follow a different curve, increasing at the beginning, reaching a peak and then gently falling.

AROMAS: These are linked to good maturation. They have different chemical structures (terpenes) and their synthesis depends primarily on the variety.

OTHER COMPOUNDS of less importance are the mineral elements, of which potassium is the most important cation, then magnesium, calcium and iron.

The table below shows the mean values of the chemical compounds in the different parts of the bunch using the Treatise of Claude Flanzy.

COMPOSITION OF THE GRAPE CLUSTER AS A PERCENTAGE OF FRESH WEIGHT

Stalks	Between 3% and 6%	Water	78 – 80
		Sugars	0.5 – 1.5
		Organic acids	0.5 – 1.6
		pH	4 – 4.5
		Tannins	2 – 7
		Minerals	2 – 2.5
		Nitrogenous compounds	1 – 1.5
Berry	Skin: 7% to 12% (mean 9.6%)	Water	78 – 80
		Organic acids	0.8 – 1.6
		Tannins	0.4 – 3
		Anthocyanins	0 – 0.5
		Nitrogenous compounds	1.5 – 2
		Minerals	1.5 – 2
		Waxes	1 – 2
		Aromatic substances	
	Seeds: between 4% and 6% (mean 4.4%)	Water	25 – 45
		Sugars	34 – 36
		Tannins	4 – 10
		Nitrogenous compounds	4 – 6.5
		Minerals	2 – 4
		Lipids	13 – 20
	Pulp: between 83% and 91%	Composition of the grape must	

COMPOSITION OF GRAPE MUST AND THE RESULTING WINE (G/L)	MUST	WINE
Water	700 – 850	750 – 900
Sugars	140 – 250	0.10 – 2
Alcohol	–	69 – 121
Organic acids	9 – 27	3 – 20
Polyphenols	0.5	2 – 6
Nitrogenous compounds	4 – 7	3 – 6
Minerals	0.80 – 2.80	0.60 – 2.50
Vitamins	0.25 – 0.80	0.20 – 0.70

THE VARIETIES AND VINE STOCKS

The vine belongs to the genus *Vitis* in the family of *Vitaceae*. The table below shows an example of taxonomic classification. *Vitis vinifera* is the most commonly cultivated species in the world, owing to the quality of its fruit either for direct consumption or for production of wines and other derivative products (raisins, aguardiente, etc.). The varieties used in wine production generally have small bunches and berries, with thin skins and small pips.

Division	Spermaphytes
Subdivision	Angiosperms
Class	Dicotyledonae
Family	Vitaceae Ampelidae
Genus	Vitis
Species	Vinifera
Variety	Tempranillo
Clone	Wine-producer's choice

Each wine-producing region is defined by a combination of varieties which have been chosen over a long period of time, based on reasons governed both by nature and by human activity. When designing a planting scheme, the choice of vine stocks is based on criteria relating to resistance to phylloxera and nematodes, resistance to limestone, resistance to drought, the affinity between variety and vine stock, the health of the vegetal material and the development as a function of the required production levels. It is an important decision and, therefore, it is necessary to be familiar with all the data relating to the soil.

DID MAN OR THE VARIETIES THEMSELVES CHOOSE THE MOST SUITABLE LANDS?

The technique of grafting is an artisanal one which is carried out either in nurseries or in the field. It involves introducing part of one plant, generally a piece of cane, into another. It is done so that the two parts, once in contact with one another, knit together and then develop as an single plant. The plant which receives the graft is called the vine stock or stock and the inserted section is called the graft or front bud.

Those varieties which are given over to producing grapes for wine are called viniferae. Broadly speaking each region supports different viniferae but some stand out and, by virtue of the ease with which they can be managed, the fineness of their wines, their colour or their bouquet, have been elevated to an important place in world oenology.

There are four basic viniferas used in red RIOJA wines: Tempranillo, Graciano, Mazuelo and Garnacha, and three in white wines: Viura, Malvasía and Garnacha Blanca. In 2008 new varieties were tried: three indigenous red varieties (Maturana Tinta, Maturana Parda and Monastel), three indigenous white varieties (Tempranillo Blanco, Maturana Blanca and Torrontes) and three non-native white varieties (Chardonnay, Verdejo and Sauvignon Blanc).

There are others but they are not significant because they form only a small proportion and do not have a definitive bearing on the quality of the wine. These varieties are distributed unevenly across the Rioja region but an idea of their distribution can be gleaned from the following table:

VARIETY	RIOJA ALTA	RIOJA ALAVESA	RIOJA BAJA	TOTAL
Tempranillo	80%	88%	68%	78%
Mazuelo	2%	1%	5%	3%
Garnacho Tinto	5%	1%	20%	11%
Graciano	1%	1%	1%	1%
Viura	9%	8%	5%	6%
Others	3%	1%	1%	1%
Total	100%	100%	100%	100%

Data from 2007

The quantity of vine stocks in each municipal district of Rioja (2007 data) is also very variable because vines are not the only crop and the districts are different sizes. Examples of districts with more than four million vines include Aldeanueva, Alfaro, Ausejo, Autol, Cenicero, San Asensio, Laguardia, Briones, San Vicente and Tudelilla, amongst others, while Alcanadre, Elciego, Haro, Labastida and Lanciego, amongst others, each have close to three million vines.

In very broad terms it is possible to identify two distinct colonies of varieties of vines for producing Rioja wine: the Tempranillo colony, or territory, is in the western area (Rioja Alta and Alavesa) and the red Garnacho territory, or colony, is in the eastern region (Rioja Baja). This division between regions has grown up over many centuries, primarily for climatic regions. The eastern, semi-arid region allows for easy production of red Garnacho which is hardier than Tempranillo, a variety which can be somewhat delicate. In contrast, the western, semi-humid region is unsuited to Garnacho because the cold weather causes problems with flowering and produces grapes of a poor colour, whereas it is easy to produce intensely coloured Tempranillo grapes.

The old estates grow both red and white varieties, producing glorious displays of mixed colours in the autumn.

88

For commercial reasons, the situation changes every year because growers dig up Garnacha and plant Tempranillo, which is an easier grape to sell commercially and is straightforward to cultivate. In view of the increasing difficulty in finding good Garnacha, La Rioja Alta, S.A. planted the "La Pedriza" estate in 2006 with some 70 ha of this variety. It is situated in the Tudelilla area of Rioja Baja and is, perhaps, the finest estate producing this variety. Garnacha has lost prestige during certain eras but it is a key variety in the production of Viña Ardanza, of which it makes up approximately 25%.

In the RIBERA DEL DUERO D.O., as well as Tempranillo (Tinto Fino), Cabernet Sauvignon, Merlot, Malbec, Garnacha Tinta and Albillo (white) are permitted. We only cultivate Tinto Fino at our estate at Áster.

In the RÍAS BAIXAS D.O. as well as Albariño which is the only variety we have planted in LAGAR DE FORNELOS, S.A., the following varieties are permitted: Caíño Blanco, Loureira, Treixadura, Torrontes and Godello (whites) and Caíño Tinto, Sousón, Mencía, Espadeira, Loureira tinta and Brancellao (reds).

> NO ONE ELEMENT SHOULD STAND OUT: THE QUALITY OF A WINE IS ROOTED IN ITS BALANCE, IN THE FUSION OF ALL ITS AROMAS AND FLAVOURS

We would like to pass on to Rioja wine lovers a simple technique for identifying varieties of vines in a vineyard. The method only applies when a grape is in the maturation period, i.e. from 10 September onwards and it is important to stress that feeling the grapes is the way to distinguish between them. The quotation *"By their fruits shall ye know them"* (Matthew 7:16) originates precisely from the difficulty in distinguishing between different grape varieties before seeing their fruits.

See below for the differentiation process:

White grape	Yellowish green berry which, when pressed in the hand, maintains its original colour for one minute.	VIURA
	Golden yellow berry which, when pressed in the hand becomes darker at the end of one minute.	MALVASIA
Red grape	External appearance of berry is grey-ash grey and, when pressed in the hand, turns from a reddish colour to brown after one minute	GRACIANO
	Reddish black berry which, when pressed in the hand, turns from red to brown after one minute.	GARNACHO/GARNACHA
	Reddish black berry which, when pressed in the hand, maintains its INTENSE reddish colour.	TEMPRANILLO
	Reddish black berry which, when pressed in the hand, maintains its PALE reddish colour.	MAZUELO

TEMPRANILLO

It is considered to be a native of Rioja, although it has spread to many of the world's wine growing regions by virtue of being considered one of the aristocratic varieties for producing wines for ageing. It is also known as Cencibel (Valdepeñas), Tinto del País (Ribera del Duero), Ull de Llebre (Catalonia), Tinto de Toro (Zamora), Tinto Fino (central Spain/Madrid), etc. The name originates from "early grape" i.e. one with a short lifecycle. It produces wines of renowned quality which bestow prestige both on the wine itself and the label. In oenological terms, it is very versatile and produces wines which are very balanced in terms of alcohol content and acidity, have relatively low polyphenol content and are smooth and fruity on the palate. It ages well in wood, yielding very complex and velvety wines, but it also adapts well to young wines and to carbonic maceration. In our group we produce Tempranillo in some of the Rioja districts famed for the quality of their wines, such as Fuenmayor, Cenicero, Rodezno, Briones, Labastida and Briñas. In Ribera del Duero we cultivate it on the Áster (Anguix) estate, which is considered one of the most suitable areas for this variety. The Tinta del País here is different to that in Rioja, producing a smaller berry with tougher skin which hinders the spread of botrytris. It produces very structured wines with more colour and polyphenol content, making them suited to long periods of ageing.

GARNACHA

This is the Spanish variety which is planted most widely in vineyards around the world. It is also cultivated in France, where it is called Grenache. It is a very hardy variety, sensitive to blight and resistant to drought and diseases such as oidium or acariosis. In Rioja it has traditionally been used as a complement to Tempranillo, being a variety which is rich in extract and has a good alcohol content. In cooler areas, such as the Rioja Alta municipalities of Badarán and Cordovín, it yields a very interesting and balanced wine which is ideal for producing rosés. Although it is a lesser known variety, it has been used in Rioja, Priorato, Ródano and Provence (Châteauneuf-du-Pape) to produce top quality wines. Our Garnacha is planted in the municipality of Tudelilla, in the La Pedriza estate which, as its name would suggest, is a very rustic and stony land which is well suited to growing this variety. It produces very structured, high quality, balanced wines of good colour and high varietal bouquet.

GRACIANO

This is a variety which requires very good climatic conditions in order to complete maturation. It is cultivated exclusively in Rioja, the region to which it is native. It was on the verge of disappearing but was saved by a few isolated stocks in vineyards in Rioja Alta (Graciano de Haro). There is also the Graciano de Alfaro variety, which is completely different. This is a variety which has a marked correlation between alcohol content and quality, so that to produce a great wine the alcohol level must reach least 12.5%. To achieve that requires very cool, clayey limestone soils such as those found on our Montecillo estate. It yields wines with a particular bouquet, which are very acidic and have a high polyphenol content, making them very suitable for ageing in barrels, blended with Tempranillo and/or Garnacha.

MAZUELO

In the Rioja D.O.C. this variety takes up about 3% of the planted vineyards. It is a very productive variety, which is very sensitive to oidium and which requires a very warm climate with plenty of sun in order to mature properly and for that reason it is generally planted in areas with guaranteed high thermals. This variety has a low aromatic profile, produces tannic wines with high acidity and stable colour and is thus a good complement to Tempranillo in long ageing wines, such as Viña Arana. It is also known as Carignan Noir in France and Cariñena in other parts of Spain.

ALBARIÑO

This variety is typical of and almost exclusive to the Rías Baixas D.O., although it is grown to some extent in Northern Portugal as Vinho Verde and in other areas, almost on an experimental basis. The most common theory is that Albariño arrived in the lands of Rías Baixas with the Cluny monks when they arrived at Salnés (Pontevedra) in the 12th century. It is highly likely that cultivation fanned out from the monastery at Armenteira (Pontevedra) throughout the valley. It has a small berry which produces a wine with a range of subtle and delicate aromas and, in years when the climate has been wet, the freshly picked fruit usually has high acidity. It has great aromatic power and a velvety character and can be relied on for a level of high quality which is reminiscent of the French Viognier. The thick skin of the grape helps it survive in the humid climate of the region where it is grown and the result is a white wine with a high alcohol content, high acidity and strong aroma. In the O Rosal region it is grown under a system of canopies and trellises. It is very vulnerable to mildew. It is the finest white variety in Spain.

MALVASÍA

This variety is not typical of a particular region. The name Malvasía refers to many different varieties. In Rioja around 60 ha are registered with the Malvasía de Rioja name. There are also others, such as the Malvasía de Sitges and Malvasía Canaria, which are genetically quite unrelated. It has a considerable capacity for producing high quality white wines. The mature bunch has reddish yellow grapes and it produces an velvety wine with an intense aroma.

VIURA

This is the main white variety grown in Rioja. It is found in the vineyards of Rioja, Catalonia (Macabeo) and, to a lesser extent, in Aragon (Alcañón). In viticultural terms, it has no specific vulnerabilities or resistances. Oenologically, it is one of the permitted varieties for Cava production. In Rioja it produces a neutral wine with high acidity and with a green taste if the grapes are not mature. Although in Rioja it is not very suited to production of young wines, it is very well suited to production of white, barrel-aged wines.

GARNACHA BLANCA

It is recognised as being of Spanish origin and may have evolved as a mutation of Garnacha Tinta. It is also known by other names, such as Grenache, Grenache blanc, Alicante blanca, Sillina blanc, Belán, Rool grenache, Garnatxa blanca, Feher grenache, etc. This variety is better adapted to hot and relatively dry climates and is prolific in Tarragona, Zaragoza and Teruel. It is the main variety in the Denominacion de Origen regions of Alella, Costers del Segre, Tarragona and Terra Alta. It produces big-bodied wines with a high alcohol content. Yellow nuances predominate and it has bouquets of ripe fruit with a bottom note of broom which confers originality. It is smooth on the palate, has moderate acidity and is slightly warm because of its high level of alcohol.

An impressive Tempranillo vine, about 35 years old, shortly before the harvest.

VITICULTURE

Bundles of American root stock, on which local varieties have been grafted, protected with paraffin wax and awaiting planting.

his chapter will look at all the different demands of a vineyard from the moment it is planted, to the decisions which need to be taken, some of which may be irreversible, to the ensuing problems which a vineyard may face. It will also consider the annual and perennial work demanded by this difficult crop, paying particular attention to the most important task, that of pruning.

PLANTING THE VINEYARD

The first stage when planning a vineyard is to carry out a preliminary study in order to determine the objectives being pursued. There are legal matters to consider, such as obtaining the rights of replanting. There are also agronomy matters, such as choosing varieties and vine stocks which are well-adapted to the area, selecting a training system and the plantation design, deciding the most suitable plantation techniques (water, laser, GPS, etc.). Lastly, there are the questions relating to a bodega's philosophy, such as the quality and quantity which it hopes to produce.

SETTING UP A VINEYARD

The first thing to determine is the conditions prevailing at the plantation site. Climate data (hours of sun, mean temperatures, rainfall patterns, rates of evapotranspiration, etc.) and data on the type of soil (texture, mineral composition, depth, etc.) are compiled. These data indicate the wine-growing ability of the land which in turn makes it possible to choose the most suitable varieties and vine stocks. These choices have legal considerations, primarily in the wine producing countries of the EU, where establishing a new vineyard is subject to legislation. Furthermore, each country regulates the varieties which are permitted in each wine producing region, determining which are recommended, which are compulsory and which are prohibited.

The choice of vine stock is based on agronomic factors, primarily resistance to phylloxera, nematodes and limestone. The only prohibition is on the use of "hybrid direct producers".

A great many graft stocks have emerged from American species of experimental hybrids. In Rioja the most commonly planted are shown on the following pages.

A "goblet" pruned vine starts to bud, outlined against a background of a glorious spring Rioja sky.
Female workers, protected by the carpet of leaves created by the vineyard's arbour, returning home after working all day at the Viña Cervera estate.

COMMON NAME	ORIGIN OF HYBRID	ACTIVE RESISTANCE TO LIMESTONE UP TO:
3.309	Riparia x Rupestres	0 – 11%
Rupestris de Lot	Rupestris de Lot variety	0 – 14%
99 R	(Richter) Berlandieri x Rupestris de Lot	0 – 17%
110 R	(Richter) Berlandieri x Rupestres	0 – 17%
161-49	Riparia x Berlandieri	0 – 25%
41-B	Chasselas (V. vinífera) x Berlandieri	0 – 50%

PLANTATION DESIGN

This is the plan which sets out how the vines will be arranged on the land. The first thing to be determined is the "plantation density", i.e. number of plants per hectare. A mean density in Rioja would be between 2,800 and 3,000 vines per hectare. The plantation design then determines the physical positioning of the plants on the land, i.e. the distances both between each vine and between the rows. Traditionally, positioning was done either in a true square frame or a staggered frame, where the distance between adjacent stocks and that between the rows was the same. The introduction of mechanised processes in vineyards has resulted in plantations being organised in lanes so that four stocks form a rectangle. A typical design in Rioja is one where there is 2.6 m between rows and 1.3 m between vines (2.6 x 1.3).

MANAGEMENT OF THE VEGETATIVE PARTS

This establishes the shape that the aerial part of the stock will take. Historically, plants were managed into a "goblet" shape consisting of a foot out of which sprouted three arms forming a triangle, with each arm containing two spurs. The La Mancha goblet is characteristically a low goblet with barely discernable arms, whilst the Rioja goblet has a taller foot with developed arms and spurs.

Modern cultivation techniques have developed through management systems which are based on posts which provide the support onto which vegetation is trained. The most well-known systems are trellises and canopies. In vertical trellises the tendrils are directed upwards along two or three horizontal wires which secure them. The arms are positioned along the lowest wire. As the tendrils grow, they are directed towards and trained along the second and third wires. Canopies allow horizontal training of the tendrils with the outer surface area being constantly exposed to the sun. The shoots form a kind of roof or covering which is about two metres off the ground. The canopies and curtains are tall arrangements which are very typical in Italy and the Rias Baixas D.O. They are more expensive and complicated to manage but they have the great advantage in very humid climates such as in Galicia. The flowers are better protected against rain during the fertilisation period, which increases the chances of successful pollination.

These systems have the advantage of offering better ventilation of bunches and greater exposure of vegetation to the sun, leading to healthier harvests and greater ripening. Furthermore, they are systems which enable greater mechanisation of the vineyard, albeit this is more the case with trellises than with canopies.

All of the above considerations form part of the studies which must be carried out when designing the plantation. The data is then used to prepare a schedule of activities which are aimed at preparing the land where the plantation will be established and these can be summarised as follows:

- Remove existing vegetation and previous crops in order to improve the health of the land
- Remove large boulders which will make working the land difficult
- Level the land
- Eliminate risk of flooding by establishing drains so as to avoid root asphyxiation
- Double dig in order to improve the soil profile and to provide a more suitable environment for plants
- Fertilise thoroughly to correct any mineral deficits
- Establish an irrigation system for future use, as and when needed
- Eliminate parasites, primarily nematodes, which transmit a great number of plant diseases

Once plantation density and the positioning of the stocks have been decided, the location of each vine is to be marked on the land. Laser beam technology has replaced the old and rudimentary plantation methods, which used string or chains and markers to determine the placement of each stock. Rows in trellis vineyards must be laid out so as to coincide with the prevailing winds in order to avoid damage later. In northern climates, the rows should be oriented north-south, or ideally north west-south east so that the leaves and the clusters receive as much sun as possible. In areas such as Germany and Switzerland rows are oriented east-west in order to take maximum advantage of the sun.

The final planting is carried out with cuttings or grafted plants protected with paraffin wax, between the end of winter and the beginning of spring, before bud break. Planting can also be carried out in pots and thus delayed until May. Subsequently, plants are given an initial watering and then are watered two or three times per week to encourage the stock to grow and become established. It is usual practice to place each foot in a plastic tube to avoid the stems being broken off by the wind or eaten by rabbits or rodents.

The vine is an annual, woody perennial which grows slowly over a number of years, following a year-on-year vegetative cycle. Each year it goes through a number of phases which recur in chronological order. The periods of the annual life cycle set out on the following pages are those found in the northern hemisphere.

The machine creates a barb with a shoot from the variety to be planted. This is introduced into the grafting stock, to which it is tied and then protected with either raffia or paraffin wax. A dibber is used to make a hole in which the pre-prepared grafted plant is placed.

The development of a vine is very striking for the speed and intensity of its growth. These two photographs, one showing a recently pruned vine and the other showing vines with plenty of vegetation, were taken only 3-4 months apart.

There are five distinct phases which occur after planting:

GROWTH AND FORMATION (I). The plant grows until it reaches its training system. This phase lasts
some three years during which no quality grapes are produced.

DEVELOPMENT OF THE PLANT (II). The plant reaches its adult state. The roots have colonised the soil
effectively. Each year the quantity of grapes produced increases, as does the quality of the harvest.
This period lasts between seven and ten years.

PRODUCTIVE PERIOD (III). Production stabilises in terms of quantity and, depending on the cultivation
techniques and the intrinsic qualities of the plant, there is a qualitative improvement in the harvest.
This period lasts about 30 years. Production per stock has increased from 0.2 kg to 2.7 kg.

WANING PERIOD (IV). The roots begin to decline, which reduces production, although quality
continues to improve albeit at a slower rate. Removal and repositioning of stocks is recommended
during this phase. Production per vine falls from 2.7 kg to 0.75 kg.

FRAGILE PHASE (V). It begins at year 55 and continues thereafter. The quantity of grapes produced by
each vine slowly decreases year by year, falling from levels which are already below 1 kg per plant.

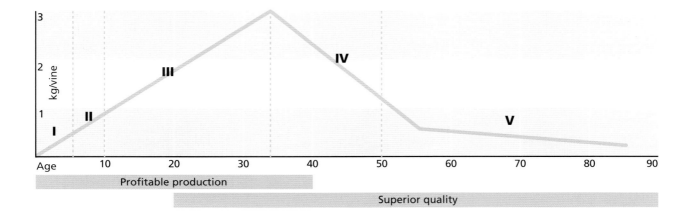

The graph shows the variations in productivity of a single vine over the course of some hundred years
as well as the variations in production which range from zero to three kilograms.

Profitability as a function of quantity can, therefore, be estimated at some forty years and, in view of
the need to recoup the considerable costs of planting, efforts have been made to shorten the stock
formation phase. Forcing productivity does however also bring forward the waning period and so
profitability is restricted to some 30 years. In any event, the dichotomy is, as in so many cases, between
quantity and quality, since profitability in terms of quantity stretches over a 40 year period whereas
maximum quality is only reached after the first 20 years.

A few days after bleeding, tiny shoots appear, on which the outlines of the leaves can already be seen.

THE ANNUAL VEGETATIVE CYCLE

Throughout the year several phases follow each other in an unchanging rhythm which is known collectively as the vegetative cycle. The following illustrates a likely annual calendar in the Rioja region:

JANUARY

THE VINE rests from November and continues in its latent condition until March when, as the ambient temperature increases, it becomes active. Pruning takes place during this period.

MARCH

BLEEDING. Once the winter rest period is over, sap pushes out through the pruning cuts and this signals the start of root activity. This phenomenon depends on the vine stock, the variety and the soil temperature (it only occurs once the soil temperature reaches some 10°C).

APRIL

DOWNING AND BUD BREAK. The leaf buds start to swell until the scales begin to separate, with a cottony mass appearing, known as down (hence the term "downing") and then subsequently a tiny green bud.

GREEN POINT. The bud continues to swell and get longer, producing a green tip which is made up of the very end of a young bud.

LEAF SPROUTING. A few very basic leaves appear, in a rosette shape; their base is still protected by the down.

EXTENDED LEAVES. The leaves are completely open and are characteristic of the variety to which they belong. Tiny tendrils emerge.

EMERGENCE OF INFLORESCENCES. The first clusters of very compact flowers appear.

SEPARATED INFLORESCENCES. The floral clusters spread out along the shoot although button-like clusters remain bunched.

SEPARATED FLORAL BUDS. The floral buds are distinctly separate from each other.

MAY-JUNE

FLOWERING. The floral cap is shed by the base bud leaving the stamens and pistils exposed.

POLLINATION. This consists of the fertilisation of the ovum by grains of pollen to produce fruit. The total failure of recently formed fruit in the cluster is known as shatter ("corrimiento"). Following fertilisation of the ovum the fruit begins to swell.

JULY

VERAISON. The young grapes change colour and texture. White grape varieties become more translucent and red ones change from a green colour to a reddish one.

SEPTEMBER/OCTOBER

RIPENING. This occurs between the middle of August and the end of September, following veraison. Major changes take place in the chemical composition of the grapes, leading to the final combination of sugars, acids, anthocyanins, phenols and aromas. The end point of this process is known as "over-ripening" at which point the berry starts to shrink as it loses water through evaporation, changing the relative concentration levels of the constituents.

NOVEMBER

WITHERING. During this phase reserves of starch build up in the old wood of the plant. The tendrils turn from green to white and then to a tobacco colour which is typical of vine shoots. The water content of the shoots falls to some 40-50%.

LEAF FALL. This marks the end of the vegetative cycle and coincides with the first cold spells of November. Absciscic acid (ABA) is formed which then leads to leaf fall.

Trimming comprises cleaning the trunk of shoots which consume energy and moisture but do not produce grapes. The vines strength can then be directed to its upper part where the bunches of grapes form.

PRUNING

Other than the harvest, the grower's biggest job of the year is pruning. As long ago as 65AD Columella in his De Re Rustica stated that pruning was a method of controlling grape quality.

The vine is a liana which would grow prolifically if left unchecked. Were this to happen, wood growth would parallel fruit production, causing erratic fruit growth of very poor quality. Pruning consists of different annual cutting operations which are carried out on shoots or trunks and it has several objectives:

- To shape the plant: goblet, canopy, trellis, etc.
- To limit the size of shoots and the vine stock frame, thereby slowing down ageing of the latter and enabling it to continue to grow in an area which is compatible with cultivation
- To regulate and balance production and the vigorousness of the stock, thereby improving the quality of the grapes and so promoting vegetation and bunch ripening, so ensuring the productive life of the vine.

Pruning can be split into two categories: dry, or winter, pruning which takes place during the period when the plant is in its latent phase, and green, or summer, pruning which is carried out during the plant's vegetative phase. One objective is to regulate the vine's production. The first step is to determine the vine's load and how it is distributed. When pruning, the pruner must, therefore, decide which part of the wood to keep and the number of buds which will remain on the stock after pruning and will form the future tendrils on the second year wood. If too small a load is left, then the production potential will be reduced, making the tendrils stronger and unbalancing the plant. On the other hand, too large a load leads to more tendrils and, therefore, more clusters, which adversely affects ripening. The following are examples of some of the pruning systems used in our area:

GOBLET PRUNING: a goblet is formed from a trunk which supports carefully spaced branches, the number of which varies and each of which generally carries spurs on which there are two buds. One example is the Rioja goblet which is formed of a trunk with three branches, each of which carries two spurs, on each of which there are two buds. This is the system traditionally used in Rioja and Ribera del Duero.

CORDON DE ROYAT PRUNING: this is a short pruning on a long frame. The horizontal part of the stock has branches spaced out in a cordon shape and trained along a wire so that the buds are alternately above or below the wire, relying on a slight twist. The cordon holds spurs with two buds. A cordon can be formed in a single direction (single cordon) or in two directions (double cordon). This is the most widely used system currently being used in Rioja and Ribera del Duero.

PARALLEL PRUNING: this is based on a very tall trunk (1.8-2 m) which is as upright as possible and has horizontal shoots and branches, which are trained along horizontal wires. This is the most widely used system in the Rias Baixas D.O. area (Albariño).

There are many other systems, such as arch pruning in Côte-Rôtie, "Mâconnais tail" pruning (taille à queue), Marne valley pruning, Chablis pruning, La Mancha, or blind, pruning, the Sylvoz pruning system, the Smart Dyson pruning system, curtain pruning, Guyot pruning, etc. It is an expensive operation which is done by hand and is very specialised. It is carried out using secateurs which can be fitted with a pneumatic system to assist with cutting. There is no feasible mechanised system for pruning although there are pre-pruners which make an initial cut which then assists and facilitates the subsequent pruning by hand.

Veraison, which is a magical and extraordinary process, is the period when the colour changes from the springtime green to the dark shades of autumn. On the same stock there may be clusters which have completed veraison and others which have not, and within the same cluster there may be red berries and green berries, an unaesthetically pleasing combination, whence comes the saying, *"If you want to hear your beloved's lamentation, take them to see the vines in veraison"*.

The regulatory body for Denominación de Origen Calificada Rioja stipulates in its regulations that the permitted pruning is twelve buds and, further, limits the total final production to 6,500 kg/hectare for red grapes and 9,000 kg/hectare for white grapes. In Ribera del Duero the maximum amount is 7,000 kg/hectare while in the Rias Baixas D.O. up to 11,000 kg/hectare is allowed for white grapes.

Is quantity the enemy of quality? Generally speaking, yes. A vine grower who decides to produce more grapes using long pruning will produce wine from those grapes which is poorer quality than he would have obtained if he had pruned in accordance with the regulations. Nevertheless, nature herself may be the cause of some outcomes which breach the regulations since in certain years the climatic conditions are so good that the grapes per hectare are bounteous and the wines excellent. This has happened in a number of years in La Rioja, including 1964, 1970, 1981, 1985, 1989, 1994, 1995, 2001 and 2005.

VINEYARD PROBLEMS AND TREATMENTS

There are various plagues and diseases which affect vineyards and these must be controlled or overcome in order to assure the quality of the grapes. The main ones are:

MILDEW (PLASMOPARA VITICOLA). This is a fungus which is known as mildew, mist or blight. Mildew affects all the green organs of the plant. Severe attacks produce partial drying of the leaves, affecting both the quality and quantity of the harvest. Prevention of this disease hinges on rapid detection in the field and cash prizes have been set up to reward vine growers who report the first spots in the field. It is combated by use of copper sulphate, used either as a pre-exposure or post-exposure prophylactic, on either a systemic basis or through contact treatment.

OIDIUM (UNCINULA NECATOR). This fungus is also known as ash, dust, blight, etc. The damage caused in the leaves is characterised by the presence of a white to ash-grey dust which, in the case of severe attacks, makes the leaves crinkly. Chocolate-coloured dotted stains appear on tendrils and canes. The clusters are covered in dust which prevents the berries from growing, causes them to crack and break and adversely affects the harvest in terms both of quantity and quality. It can be controlled through either pre-exposure or post-exposure prophylaxis, with sulphur dusting being one of the most common treatments on account of its efficacy and low cost.

GREY ROT (BOTRYTIS CINEREA). This fungus is commonly known as botrytis, gangrene, rot, etc. In the bunches the most serious attacks occur between veraison and harvest; the most vulnerable varieties are those with very compact clusters and berries with very thin skins. Typically the clusters appear rotten and develop a greyish mold on the surface. The damage causes loss of the harvest, both in terms of quantity and quality, with colour being adversely affected, aroma being lost, etc. This disease must be fought with chemicals and the best form of control is by applying a preventative "standard system". Furthermore, cultural attitudes are important, for example not over-using nitrogenous fertilizers, or carrying out balanced pruning, removing shoots, burning pruned materials, etc., all help prevent this disease.

GRAPE MOTH (LOBESIA BOTRANA). This insect which overwinters hidden in the bark of the vines, in the earth, in leaves, etc. The second generation causes damage in the grape bunches, leading to wounds in the berries which encourages rotting. It is combated by using mating disruption techniques.

YELLOW SPIDER (TETRANYCHUS URTICAE). This damages plants by making holes in the leaves which then die. It also attacks the berries, causing similar symptoms to those of oidium.

ACARIOSIS (CALEPITRIMERUS VITIS). This damages tendrils (causing delayed bud break) and leaves (white spots develop which can be seen against the light). It causes the flowers in the buds to abort leading to low levels of pollination and thus to a reduction in the harvest.

NEMATODE DISEASES. The significance of these diseases lies in the damage that they cause to the roots through the transmission of viruses, thereby adversely affecting the quantity and quality of the harvest.

DAMAGE CAUSED BY BIRDS, RABBITS, HARES AND SNAILS. They peck at or bite the grapes, causing wounds which then rot. They also damage the plant, the grapes and the harvest. The solution is to protect the vineyard with systems to stop them gaining access to the vines.

DAMAGE CAUSED BY HIGH TEMPERATURES. These cause leaves and bunches to dry out, and thus the loss of the harvest, when temperatures exceed 42°C. The vine cannot survive when exposed to temperatures above 55°C.

DAMAGE CAUSED BY LOW TEMPERATURES. These occur most frequently as a result of frosts which, if they are early, only affect the young buds, meaning that a second bud break can occur from the secondary buds. In such cases the shoots affected by the frost can be removed by green pruning and a second bud break expected, but this is not normally of the quality needed for great wines. Vines can tolerate winter temperatures of up to 20° below zero.

DAMAGE CAUSED BY HAIL AND RAIN. These may occur between spring and summer and cause breaks and wounds in the shoots, leaves and grapes.

DAMAGE CAUSED BY WIND. This causes the shoots to snap and tears off leaves and clusters.

A bunch of grapes affected by botrytis cinerea, a very real problem in many parts of the world, but which has also produced some truly remarkable wines in regions such as Sauternes and Tokaji.

It is autumn and beneath a sky which threatens storms - the greatest fear of any farmer - the harvest is being gathered in boxes in Torre de Oña, S.A.

RIPENING
AND HARVEST

The harvest in O Rosal, being ahead of that in Cambados, faces less risk of storms and a greater chance of good ripening.

LAGAR DE FORNELOS, S.A.

O' ROSAL

he harvest is, without doubt, the most exciting moment of the year – it is the moment of truth, the reward or punishment for all our labours ... with a sprinkling of luck from the weather gods. This chapter will look at the grape ripening process up to harvest and at the different harvesting methods.

GRAPE RIPENING PROCESS

Wines need to have certain minimum concentration levels of sugar, acidity, aromas, anthocyanins and TPI (Total Polyphenol Index, a spectrometric measurement of colour) before they can be aged in barrel and bottle. To produce a wine with sufficient concentrations of the above constituents, the raw material must have adequate concentrations of them and it must also be possible to extract them during the vinification process. There are various factors on which this depends:

GEOLOGICAL AND CLIMATIC FACTORS. The climate conditions, the composition of the soil and the drainage facilities are all very important in determining the concentration of phenol compounds in the grape berry and, thus, in the wine. This is the concept of "terruño", or terroir, and it explains why the same variety of vinifera may yield distinctly different wines in different locations. Two other very important influences on grape ripening are how fertile the land is and how much water is available. Both factors determine the eventual vigorousness of the plant and its productivity and thereby the quality of the grape and the wine which is ultimately produced.

GENETIC FACTORS. The variety of vinifera also affects the quality of the grape and the wine. This is firstly, because the size of the berry determines the ratio between skin and volume of must. Varieties with small berries have a greater surface area to weight ratio and will, therefore, have a larger surface area for exchange during vinification. For this reason, varieties with small berries are generally the more valued in production of high-quality red wines, as they produce a better colour and overall concentration.

CULTURAL FACTORS. The training and pruning systems, the planting density and fertilisers and irrigation all affect the yield per vine and the concentration of phenol compounds in the grape.

Production of high quality red wines requires yields to be limited to reasonable levels; where yields are too high, there is insufficient raw material with adequate concentrations of phenol compounds. One point to be borne in mind is that high yields generally affect phenol concentrations more than sugar concentrations.

The process of ripening influences the concentrations of sugars and acids in the berry and also has an important effect on the molecules responsible for the colour and aromas which determine the quality of the wine. During the final stages of the process of ripening, sugars accumulate and phenol compounds are actively synthesised and there are certain other changes which affect the quality of the wine.

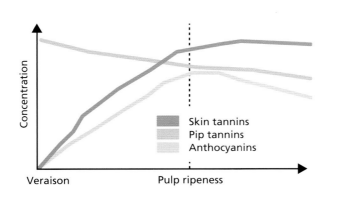

The graph shows the concentrations of anthocyanins and tannins in the grape throughout the process of ripening (Ribéreau-Gayon et al., 1999). It can be seen that the concentration of anthocyanins increases during ripening up to a peak level, after which it falls away slightly. The level of tannins in the skin rises as the level of tannins in the pips falls. Tannins are responsible for the astringency of a wine and it is, therefore, very interesting to look at their levels throughout the ripening process. It then becomes clear that the correct degree of ripening is critical in producing quality wines.

Another important factor to be borne in mind is that the degree of ripening of the grape affects both colour extraction during vinification and fixing of different compounds in the wine, in such a way that these are not lost during barrel ageing.

PULP RIPENESS AND PHENOLIC RIPENESS

In 1999 Ribéreau-Gayon established the term "phenolic ripeness", as opposed to the classic "pulp ripeness". This latter, which is the maximum ratio between sugar and total acidity, may be a perfectly valid way of determining the date for the harvest for white wine but it is not a correct reference point with regard to red wines, since the ripeness of the seeds and the skin does not necessary correlate with pulp ripeness. In this case it is more appropriate to use the concept of "phenolic ripeness".

Curve 1 shows an example of early phenolic ripening, i.e. preceding pulp ripening. This happens when a variety is maladapted to the geological and climatic conditions. It will be necessary to harvest before pulp ripening is completed and to correct the likely alcohol content in the bodega. This situation arises in wines from certain regions which are rich in colour and tannicity but in which chaptalizing (adding sugar to increase the alcohol content) is almost indispensible. Curve 2 shows an example of a variety which is well adapted to the terroir, with phenolic and pulp ripening taking place at the same time. It is advisable to try and select those varieties which best conform to Curve 2. Curve 3 shows an example of late phenolic ripening. A certain degree of over-ripening of the pulp is required in order to allow the skin and seeds to mature correctly. This happens with some varieties and in some vine-growing regions where, in order to achieve the correct phenolic ripeness, it is necessary to delay to a point where a very high alcohol content is likely. Lastly, Curve 4 shows an example of overly late phenolic ripening and is a case of inadequate ripening resulting from geological and climatic conditions which are unsuited to production of quality wines.

Establishing phenolic ripeness is extremely useful in deciding the date of the harvest, in deciding a bodega's in-house classification as a function of the level of quality and even in making it possible, by means of established vinification methodology, to affect the level of extraction. Nevertheless, it must be noted that putting in place a system for deciding the date of the harvest as a function of monitoring phenolic ripeness is in reality complicated by the fact that there are considerable differences in collecting samples and in the protocol for grape maceration.

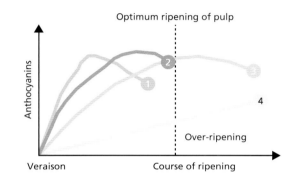

Once samples have been collected and analysed, data obtained from visits to the various plots of land during the current year and previous years has been considered and the meteorological forecast has been taken into account, the ideal date for starting the harvest can be determined.

THE HARVEST

The harvest is a very important operation which accounts for approximately 40% of the annual outlay, in terms both of man hours and financial costs. The first step, which is determined some months in advance, is to decide which methodology will be used. Each plot of land is unique and so the most suitable harvesting system must be established in order to pick the grapes in the best conditions (manual or mechanical, in boxes, crates or trailers, etc.). An estimate of the size of the harvest is also made (kilos per hectare, kilo per vine and total kilos from the harvest). At La Rioja Alta, S.A. and its subsidiaries, the preliminary estimate governs one, very important, operation aimed at reducing the yield per hectare to levels which will lead to a better quality of grapes. This operation is known as "bunch thinning" (some bunches are removed so that the remaining bunches ripen better) and it is very expensive, in terms both of hours of work (it takes about

Spontaneous photographs are difficult to take but this one shows some of the grape pickers on the Viña Cervera estate.

Maceration of the pulp and the skins, to maximise colour extraction, is an important part of ripeness monitoring when determining the ideal date for starting the harvest.

the same time as the harvest itself) and of lost produce, since in some years up to 40% of the grapes may be removed. In many cases precise pruning in winter can avoid such overproduction.

Once the likely volume of the harvest has been established, the number of workers and grape pickers needed are decided, based on the assumption that one grape picker harvesting manually is able to collect between 800 and 1,000 kilos per 8 hour working day.

Another important aspect to take into account is the distance between the vineyard and the bodega as this will set the rhythm of deliveries and will determine how many "workers" will be needed. It is thought that a distance which can be covered in about half an hour is the maximum acceptable to avoid damage to the grapes.

From veraison onwards, the technical staff begin monitoring and assessing the different plots of land with the aim of determining the date of the harvest. This is the most important decision of the year and will be the

SETTING THE DATE
FOR THE HARVEST IS
THE MOST IMPORTANT
DECISION OF THE YEAR

based on analysis of the various results. For this reason, weekly analyses of the concentrations of sugar, acidity and phenol and aromatic compounds are carried out. Historically, plots of land were chosen as a function of the homogeneity of the grapes (age of the vineyard, variety, topography, soil and historical analysis of the wines produced). Samples of, say, 200 grapes are collected from different vines in each of the plots of land so that the overall sample can be as representative as possible.

Once the date of the harvest has been decided, the pre-determined plan is implemented, with grape pickers being contracted, the harvest materials being stocked (boxes, baskets, harvest knives "corquetes" or secateurs, safety equipment), with the necessary machinery being overhauled and all the equipment which will come into contact with the grapes being rigorously cleaned.

The vessels into which the harvest is placed are a key aspect in safeguarding the condition of the grapes. Traditionally, the grapes were transported on the backs of donkeys in wooden, truncated, cone-shaped vessels called "comportones" (trugs). Later, trailers pulled by animals were used and these then gave way to mechanical tractors. The trailers must be able to ensure that the grapes remain intact and avoid any damage and crushing which would produce readily oxidable musts and they are, therefore, made of stainless steel and with a maximum depth of 75 cm.

At La Rioja Alta, S.A., the harvest is collected in plastic crates capable of holding 350 kg of grapes which are placed on the trailers which then travel round the "ranks" or rows in the vineyard, with the grape pickers carefully loading the harvested bunches. The crates are then loaded into refrigerated lorries to be transported to the bodega, where they are unloaded.

At the Torre de Oña, Aster and Lagar de Cervera bodegas, the harvest is collected in 20 kg capacity plastic crates which are placed around the vineyard. The grape pickers harvest the grapes and place them into the crates which are then transported to the bodega in refrigerated lorries. Once at the

Manual sorting of Tempranillo in Áster, to remove leaves, impurities and under-ripe grapes.

bodega, the grapes are weighed and put through a rigorous quality control process which will shape the destiny of the resulting wines. This is the point at which the regulatory bodies for the different Denominaciones de Origen determine the quality, quantity and provenance of the delivered grapes.

There are two main types of harvest:

MANUAL HARVEST. Using "corquetes" and/or secateurs the grape pickers cut the bunches and place them in baskets or crates which are then emptied into or loaded onto trailers and then transported back to the bodega. Where the harvest is collected in crates, it remains in the crates whilst being transported back to the bodega where it is then put onto a selection table and the damaged grapes or those in poor condition removed. It is an expensive operation but it improves the quality of the harvest.

MECHANICAL HARVEST. The first machine appeared in France in 1971 and, since then, there has been a considerable increase in mechanisation throughout the wine producing world. The lateral shaking system is the most commonly used. The harvest is carried out using tractors which move up and down the rows in the vineyard, shaking the stems of the vines and dislodging the grapes into containers which are then transported to the bodega, with the stalks remaining on the plants. It is a quick operation, is cheaper than a manual harvest and is gaining in popularity, particularly in hot regions where it is sometimes carried out at night (a "nocturnal harvest"), with the advantage that the grapes arriving at the bodega are cool. This harvesting method has been applied to every type of training system, from high goblets to parallel systems, although it is most suited to vertical systems (trellises). This method of collecting the grapes requires swift transportation to the bodega, since it produces a high number of damaged grapes and, thus, a higher quantity of readily oxidable must.

As the harvest draws to an end on a sunny day, it is time to relax and celebrate.

The clean wine passes through the drum of a horizontal press. It is a wine with a stronger colour and greater intensity than free run wine but it is also somewhat more astringent. The oenologist will decide whether it is to be used or sold.

OENOLOGY

Since the 2006 harvest, malolactic fermentation has been carried out in barrels at both Barón de Oña and Áster.

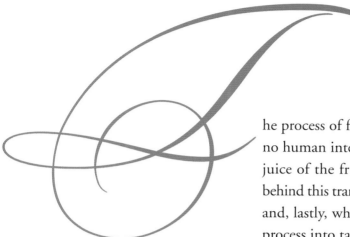

he process of fermentation is a magical one which takes place with almost no human intervention, with sugar turning naturally into alcohol and the juice of the fruit into wine. This chapter will briefly set out the science behind this transformation, the problems which may arise and their solutions and, lastly, what machinery is needed in a bodega to turn this mysterious process into tangible success.

ALCOHOLIC FERMENTATION AND YEASTS

Oenology was born with the first discoveries in the world of microbiology by the Dutchman Antoni van Leeuwenhoeck who, midway through the 17th century and using a homemade microscope, observed the microorganisms of must in fermenting grapes. During the 19th century Louis Pasteur, after a mere four years of intensive laboratory investigations, discovered alcohol fermentation and in a simple fashion demonstrated the correlation between yeasts and this biochemical process, obtaining pure cultures of the different yeasts, from which he studied their origins. Other scientists (for example Alexandre Guilliermond, in France, and Winge, in Denmark) discovered that lemon-shaped cells (apiculate yeasts) predominate in the initial phase of the spontaneous fermentation of grape must. As fermentation progresses these apiculate yeasts give way to other, elliptical-shaped yeasts which are then deposited at the bottom, once all the sugars in the must have been taken up.

The name "fermentation" (from the Hebrew "fervere") was initially given to the phenomenon of decomposition of organic material whereby there was a rapid and violent release of gases. These are chain reactions catalysed by microbial enzymes and the final result will depend on the physiological particularities of each yeast, the composition of the must and the ambient conditions in which the reaction takes place.

In biochemistry terms, it is a process in which the glucose in the must is converted firstly into pyruvic acid, is then reduced to ethanol such that one molecule of glucose is converted into two molecules of ethanol and two molecules of CO_2, thereby releasing heat. Thus, every 180 grams of sugar will produce 92 grams of ethanol and 88 grams of carbon dioxide.

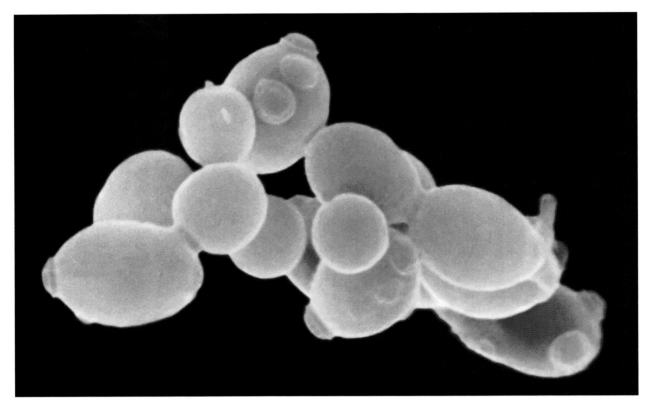

Electronic microscope photograph of Saccharomyces cerevisiae yeast, which is responsible for converting the sugar in the grapes into alcohol. Sample report of analysis of a wine, in this case a batch which will make up the Viña Ardanza 2005 coupage, before bottling.

Not all the sugar molecules in the must behave in accordance with the preceding equation. Depending on the metabolism of the yeast, a certain number of molecules will be converted into two other, very important compounds. One of these is glycerine, the third biggest constituent of wine after water and ethanol. Glycerine is attributable to the characteristics of smoothness and structure of a wine. The other important compound is pyruvic acid. Pyruvic acid is the source of further group of secondary compounds, namely acetic acid, which has a negative impact on any wine and whose levels must be kept low, and diacetyl and acetoin, which at certain concentrations may damage the aroma of the wine.

Yeasts are also capable of metabolising other compounds in the must, such as nitrogenous compounds. These are involved in the synthesis of higher alcohols (isoamyl and isobutyl alcohol), which at low concentrations improve the aroma of the wine but at high concentrations (above 400 mg/l) lead to unpleasant aromas.

Furthermore, yeasts can break down compounds which contain sulphur, such as the sulphur contained in the skin of grapes as a result of chemical treatments and which may be converted into hydrosulphuric acid which will give the wine an unpleasant aroma of "rotten eggs".

MONITORING ALCOHOLIC FERMENTATION

The graph is a typical representation of wine fermentation showing three distinct phases.

The first phase, (a), is the latency phase, during which there is a low number of yeasts originating in the grape and the bodega machinery. The yeasts become acclimatised to the new medium and, depending on the must and the ambient conditions in the bodega, this phase lasts between one and five days.

The second phase, (b), shows an exponential growth, with the yeasts multiplying rapidly, various generations of cells being produced and the predominant genus, Saccharomyces cerevisiae, being the only one capable of surviving the alcohol which it is generating. Sugars are rapidly converted, causing a swift increase in temperature and a considerable quantity of CO_2 to be released.

FERMENTATION CURVES

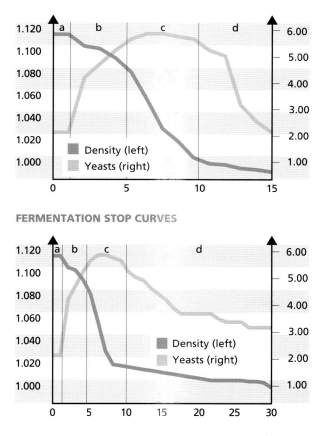

FERMENTATION STOP CURVES

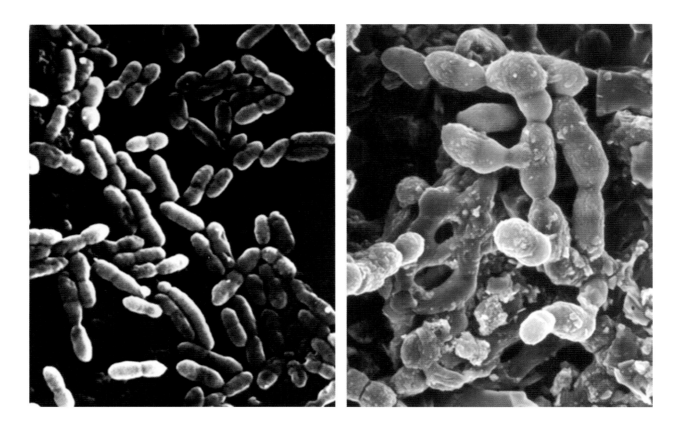

Electron microscope images of lactic bacteria (bacilli and cocci), responsible for malolactic fermentation, photographed inside a barrel.

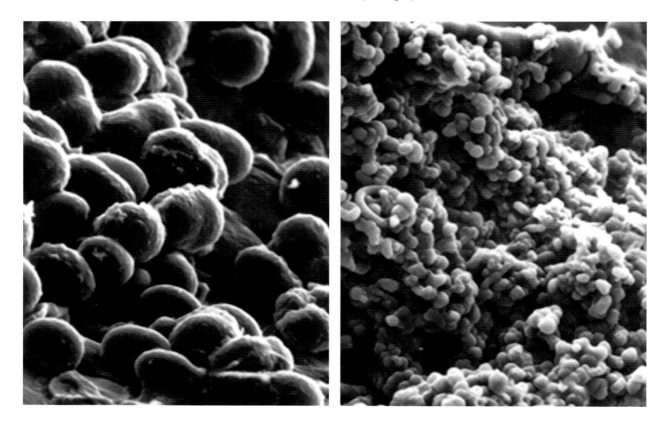

Phase (c) is the end of fermentation which coincides with a drop in the amount of yeasts, which reduces the amount of sugar and is brought about by the inhibitory effect of the alcohol produced. This phase is considered to be at an end when the sugar concentration in the wine is below 3 g/l.

Certain problems can arise during this stage, such as fermentation slowing down or stopping. When fermentation slows down, sugars are fermented less quickly or the process may indeed stop completely, leaving wines which contain sugar which has not yet been converted. This sugar is vulnerable to attacks from other microorganisms which may modify the wine being produced (cf. fermentation stop curve graph on the previous page).

This problem can be prevented by knowing the precise composition of the must, so that deficits in certain compounds can be corrected by adding them, such as vitamins, nitrogenous compounds and crusts of dead yeasts which provide the sterols and fatty acids which are necessary for cells to multiply and which are able to fix substances which inhibit yeast growth. If fermentation stops, it may be restarted by using selected yeasts which are able to survive in this medium and convert the remaining sugars into alcohol.

MALOLACTIC FERMENTATION

The first references to this process date from 1894 when Fleurieu and Ordedonneau observed that malic acid levels drop during the ageing of wine. It was not, however, until 1901 that Kunz proved that this drop in malic acid levels is accompanied by a simultaneous increase in lactic acid levels. In the mid 20th century an increase

COCCI	BACILII
Pediococcus pentosaceus	Lactobacillus plantarum
Pediococcus parvulus	Lactobacillus uvarum
Pediococcus damnosus	Lactobacillus casei
Leuconostoc mesenteroides	Lactobacillus hilgardii
Oenococcus oeni	Lactobacillus fructivorans

in microbiology research in Italy and France resulted in the discovery that this conversion is due to certain bacteria, now known as lactic bacteria as they ultimately generate lactic acid. These bacteria form a heterogeneous group with certain general characteristics, namely that they are rounded (cocci) or elongated (bacilli), are able to ferment sugars and which, when stained using the Gram method and then observed through a microscope, are blue (Gram positive).

From a biochemical perspective, this is not strictly a fermentation but rather a biological process of acid correction in which malic acid in wine is converted by bacteria into lactic acid, with Oenococcus oeni being recognised as being the most representative of this reaction.

In an overall reaction, 134 g malic acid is converted into 90 g lactic acid and 44 g CO_2, or, put another way, 1 g malic acid forms 0.67 g lactic acid and approximately 167 cm^3 of CO_2. The main results of this process in the wine are a fall in acidity levels, an improvement in the organoleptic qualities and a defence against the possibility of microbiological contamination.

There is one principle which has already become an article of faith for red wines which are rich in

The vats, whether wooden, concrete or stainless steel, are filled with grapes.

Shortly afterwards, a paste is formed from the skins and pips; this rises to the top and forms what is known as the cap, or "sombrero".

As must ferments and undergoes remontage, alcohol levels, colour and aromas all increase.

The wine is racked into a fresh barrel to undergo malolactic fermentation.

malic acid and are going to be aged and that is to watch for malolactic degradation and ensure that it coincides with or immediately follows alcohol fermentation.

In the case of white wines, however, this decision is more arbitrary, depending primarily on the characteristics sought in the final product. If it is a question of maintaining fruitiness and the young and fresh character of a varietal wine, such fermentation may be damaging. If, however, volume, roundness and character are sought, it may be advisable. It is, ultimately a technical decision whether or not to use this technique, or use it to a certain degree as is the case in the production of certain white wines in which the acid characteristic may vary from one harvest to another. It is, therefore, advisable to be familiar with the advantages and disadvantages of the technique and to consider them in the light of the wine to be produced. In Lagar de Cervera, for example, partial malolactic fermentation is carried out, with the percentage being determined as a function of the factors of each harvest.

ADVANTAGES	DISADVANTAGES
Reduction in acidity	Reduction in colour
Microbiological stability	Reduction in varietal aromas
Increase in a wine's aromas	Increase in volatile acidity
Reduction in bitterness and astringency	Emergence of anomalous flavours and smells
Complexity and ageing capability	Histamine formation

The above table sets out some of the advantages and disadvantages of malolactic acid correction in wines.

WINE-MAKING PROBLEMS

An alteration is a change to the normal chemical composition of the wine and may be of either chemical or microbiological origin. The latter are traditionally known as "diseases of wine" because of the Pasteurian criterion applied to the term "disease", with the former being classified as "alterations".

CHEMICAL ALTERATIONS

OXIDATION. This happens when the wine comes into contact with oxygen in the air, causing chemical oxidation of ethanol into acetaldehyde, which has a smell reminiscent of sherry. This alteration can be avoided by keeping the wine in air-tight conditions, ensuring that there are no air voids in the vats and maintaining appropriate dosing of sulphur dioxide.

METALLIC SPOILING. A high content of metals such as iron and copper may cause clouding in bottled wine; this is known respectively as ferric and copper spoiling. There are many and various reasons for an excess of these metals, some of which have been identified as chemical treatments, pipes, iron deposits, etc.

PROTEIN SPOILING. This occurs in those white wines which are rich in insoluble proteins. When the proteins react with the tannins in the wine or with substances transferred from the cork stopper, they produce a whitish hazy precipitate in the bottled wine. It can be prevented by clarifying the wine before bottling.

DISEASES IN WINE

YEAST DISEASES:

WINE FLOR. When a wine suffers this alteration, fine flecks appear on the surface of the vessels (vats or barrels) containing the wine. The flecks then coalesce until the surface of the wine is covered, firstly in a smooth flat layer and subsequently an increasingly thick and uneven one. The flor develop in wines with low alcohol contents especially young wines which are in contact with ambient oxygen. This alteration causes the wine to smell like glue (ethyl acetate) which, if not corrected, may cause all the wine to be lost through vinegarisation. Such flor can be avoided by keeping the wine in airtight conditions and maintaining correct levels of sulphur dioxide preservative. One traditional practice in the bodegas is to put small bowls containing a solution of potassium metabisulphite and citric acid onto the surface of vessels containing wine so that it releases sulphur dioxide into the void, thereby preventing the flor from proliferating. One positive application of such flor is the production of wines using biological ageing in the Jerez region.

REFERMENTATION. This occurs in wines which contain unfermented sugars. Fermentation of these remaining sugars begins in the absence of oxygen, such as in bottled wines. It causes cloudiness and releases large amounts of CO_2 which may cause the wine to spill out of the bottle if the stopper is forced out or, in the worst cases, the glass shatters. This alteration can be avoided by bottling with low residual sugar levels, keeping the wine carefully in cool temperatures and adding yeast growth inhibitors. One outstandingly positive application of this alteration is the traditional method of producing sparkling wines, with French Champagne and Cava from Catalonia being the most obvious examples.

BRETTANOMYCES GENUS, better known as "brett". This is a yeast which causes contamination which in turn affects the olfactory characteristics of the wine, producing aromas of animal and old leather which at professional tastings are described as "smell of horse sweat, barnyard or stables" for red wines and "ink or solvent" for white wines. The compounds responsible for the smell are 4-ethylphenol and 4-ethylguaiacol. This alteration can appear at any stage in production and tends to occur more often during ageing in oak, primarily when the wood of the barrel is not cleaned correctly. One method of preventing it is to maintain a strict regime of barrel cleaning, which will prevent or minimise growth of these germs.

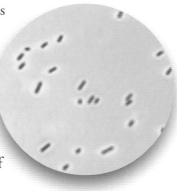

Yeasts

MILDEW DISEASES:

GREY ROT IN THE GRAPE. The cause of this disease is a fungus, Botrytis cinerea, which during rainy summers and damp autumns attacks the grapes, breaks through the skin and into the grape, causing the juice to be lost and thus a considerable reduction in the harvest. Wines made from rotten grapes darken when exposed to air, turning to chocolate colours. Moreover, mouldy and bitter aromas develop and these later appear in the wine, causing a drop in the quality of the harvest. One positive application of this alteration is the wines of Sauternes and Tokaji.

Fungi

BACTERIAL DISEASES:

INFECTIONS CAUSED BY ACETIC BACTERIA. These bacteria cause oxidation of the ethanol in wine when it comes into contact with oxygen. This disease is the most damaging and difficult to resolve. When the disease is in its early stage and affects only the surface layers of the container it is called "souring" but, as it develops and intensifies, it affects the entire contents of the container and is then called "vinegarisation", which is in fact the basis of industrial vinegar production. This alteration can be avoided by preventing the must or the wine coming into contact with oxygen in the air and by maintaining adequate levels of sulphur dioxide.

Bacteria

INFECTIONS CAUSED BY LACTIC BACTERIA . These alterations are linked by the fact of their being caused by a group of bacteria which are present in the wine, which develop in the absence of oxygen and which have nowadays been virtually eradicated thanks to improvements in the methods of preserving musts and wines, so leaving these infections to the footnotes of history.

This section will consider a series of treatments which can be carried out on musts with the objective of correcting certain defects in their composition, whether in a permanent manner relating to specific geographic conditions, or on an interim basis owing to possible climatological conditions. These methods are legal and are regulated by competent organisations so as to avoid fraud and alterations which may pose a danger to human health. The chapter on bottling will cover corrections in wine. There are two different types:

CHAPTALISATION. This is named after Napoleon's Minister of the Interior, the scientist Jean-Antoine Chaptal. It is used to increase the alcohol content in wines when the desired level has not been reached and it entails adding sugar from other crops to the must, for example from sugar beet or cane sugar. In empirical terms, between 16 and 18 grams of sucrose per litre produces 1 degree of alcohol expressed by volume. It is also possible to use concentrated grape must. On the other hand, there are techniques which can be used to concentrate the constituents of a must, by eliminating water, amongst which concentrators and inverse osmosis systems are the most notable. The wines become more concentrated but they lose elegance, refinement and sophistication. This practice is illegal in the D.O.s where we have wineries and we support this ban.

ACIDIFICATION. This entails adding an organic acid to increase the fixed acidity of the must or wine. The most widely used is tartaric acid, with 1 gram per litre of tartaric acid producing an increase of 0.65 g/l in the fixed acidity. Other permitted acids are citric acid, ascorbic acid and lactic acid, whilst use of strong acids such as sulphuric acid or hydrochloric acid is banned.

ACID CORRECTION. This entails reducing the fixed acid in the musts or the wines. It can be carried out either by means of biological acid correction using lactic bacteria or by using chemical products such as calcium carbonate, neutral potassium tartrate and potassium bicarbonate.

INSTALLATIONS IN THE BODEGA

These are the equipment and materials used in the conversion of grapes into must and in preserving and storing of wines. The principle ones shall be considered.

CONTAINERS

Their origins stretch back in time to the moment when Man progressed from eating grapes fresh from the vine to producing and storing wine, constructing receptacles initially from materials such as stone and clay. The "stone vats" of Rioja Alavesa and Rioja Alta may even be the last descendents of those first containers. It is thought that the first vessels specifically made for wine were either clay or earthenware,

After the first fermentation, the clean wine is removed to a container and the residue (skins and pips) are emptied into a container to be taken to the presses.

although their fragility prevented them being made to hold large quantities. They were shaped like upturned pears, with wide mouths which made them difficult to seal, and there are still examples of them at some bodegas in La Mancha.

The next vessels to appear were made from various kinds of wood, such as oak, chestnut, ash, etc. The smaller wooden vessels were known as barrels (200-300 litres) and the larger ones as vats. The hogsheads have the shape of horizontal barrels, have different capacities and historically were used as containers for transportation. They are made preferably from oak because of its capacity to be worked and its inherent water tightness.

WOODEN CONTAINER	CAPACITY
Vat	> 1000 litres
Hogshead	500 litres
Bordeaux barrel	225 litres
Burgundy barrel	228 litres

Later, after containers made of fired clay and wood, came those made of reinforced concrete which were used widely on account of their thermal inertia and which were later improved by being coated with epoxy resins. Finally, came the turn of stainless steel containers, which are cylindrical, can be of any capacity and have hermetic and hygiene properties which make them eminently suitable for use in a bodega. Nevertheless, at the end of the 20th century, wooden barrels made a strong come-back.

Whether a container is made of wood, concrete or stainless steel, it will have various accessories, such as upper and front covers, wine or must outlet apertures and sample and level taps.

CIRCULATION PUMPS

Movement of liquids in a bodega requires a propelling force, which may be gravity where there are sufficient differences in levels or else mechanical pumps. The latter are responsible for bringing up and transporting liquids from one place to another, without changing the characteristics of those liquids. There are various types:

PISTON PUMP. This consists of one or more pistons which move within cylinders in an alternating in/out movement which enables large amounts of liquids to be moved. It is an indispensible pump in bodegas, not least because it enables both paste and clean or dirty wines to be moved.

DIAPHRAGM PUMP. This works in a very similar manner to the piston pump. It consists of a metal or rubber membrane which is made to flex, thereby drawing in and then expelling liquid. It is used to move clean wines.

PERISTALTIC PUMP. This is the most recent arrival in the wine-making industry. It comprises an interior membrane through which the liquid circulates; the membrane is compressed by an impeller situated on the outside of the membrane, thereby moving the wine. It is used to move delicate wines, so as to avoid them losing any of their characteristics.

OTHER PUMPS used in the wine-making industry are impeller pumps, gear pumps, Mohno pump, centrifugal pumps, etc.

Presses have changed very little since wine was first produced. There are vertical or horizontal systems, some more technical than others, but they all include systems for collecting the wine remaining in the skins without exerting too much pressure, so as to protect the quality.

These comprise a combination of machines, which are tailor-made to suit the characteristics of each bodega. The most important ones are the sampling tools, the hoppers for unloading grapes, the wine piping systems, the selection conveyor belts or tables, the destemmers, the juice extractors, the grape-solids pumps and, lastly, the presses, which are sufficiently important in oenological terms as to merit some explanation.

The first presses date from the Egyptian and Greek civilisations which used systems involving treading grapes by foot; these then evolved into beam presses and much later into the modern day vertical plate press. The principle is based on extracting the must or wine from the solid parts of the harvest, be it fresh grapes (white wines) or recently fermented skins (red wines), by exerting both vertical and horizontal pressure. The liquid is then collected in troughs and then transported to vats to start fermentation or to be stored. There are various types of presses:

VERTICAL. These are the oldest type but are still very widely used because they produce high quality must or wine. They comprise a grooved wood or metal container into which the harvest is emptied and is then pressed by a plate which moves down over it, forcing liquid out through the grooves of the container.

HORIZONTAL. These comprise a horizontal cylinder with two plates inside. The harvest is put in between the two plates, which move towards one another via a screw located on the axle, compressing the grapes and forcing the liquid out through grooves in the cylinder.

MEMBRANE PRESS. These are similar to the above presses except that the two internal plates are replaced by a central flexible membrane which is filled with either water or air, thereby compressing the harvest and so forcing the liquid out through the grooved cylinder.

TEMPERATURE AND HUMIDITY CONTROL

Traditionally, cool temperatures were used in bodegas to create good storage conditions for the wines in underground areas where temperatures were lower and more stable than those at ground level. However, when bodegas became more industrialised, it became necessary to install mechanical systems, such as air conditioning equipment and heat pumps which enable monitoring to ensure the correct temperature and humidity conditions.

There are many ways in which temperature is controlled within a bodega but particularly important are the cooling of the must prior to racking, the process of alcohol fermentation, stabilising of tartaric precipitates, fitting out of the premises for ageing and storing wine, etc. Furthermore, heat can be used to start off alcohol and/or malolactic fermentation if these do not start spontaneously because the must or wine is at too low a temperature.

There are three areas within a bodega where it is essential to control ambient humidity, namely the area containing the wooden fermentation vats, the area for ageing in barrels and the labelling area. The relative humidity in the air affects levels of wastage produced during the time that the wine is in barrels and also the composition of the wine. If the relative humidity in areas housing wooden containers is low, then there will be wastage (approximately 2% per annum in normal circumstances) by way of water loss through the staves. In contrast, where humidity is high (90-95%), wastage and the alcohol content of the wine are both lower because of condensation of ambient water. To maintain the areas for ageing at suitable relative humidity levels, either the ground is kept lightly watered or, by preference, ambient humidifiers are used.

The original La Rioja Alta, S.A. bodega of 1890. These 100 year old vats were used for fermentation until the 1996 harvest. Today they are kept full of wine, with the aim of keeping them in good condition.

New fermentation equipment fitted with the most up-to-date technology at the Rioja Alta, S.A. bodega in Labastida. In the background is Haro.

PRODUCTION

The start of the harvest at La Rioja Alta, S.A.. The grapes are collected in crates and then quickly transported to the bodega.

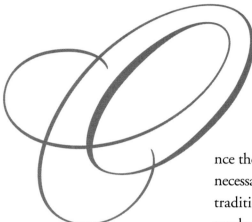nce the essential information regarding fermentation is established, it is then necessary to start to specialise according to the type of wine to be made, regional traditions, the variety of grape, the historical era, etc. Details of the main production techniques, i.e. for reds, whites and rosés, are set out below, as are brief details of other, very special, techniques practised elsewhere in the world.

PRODUCTION OF RED WINES

Red wine is a wine which undergoes maceration, in which the alcohol fermentation of the must takes place at the same time as the components of the solid parts of the grape are broken down. These "noble components", which are found in the skins and the pips (and also in the stalk), are known as polyphenols and belong to two families of chemical compounds with very complex structures, namely tannins and anthocyanins. The condition of the skins is very important in the harvest, both in terms of quality and quantity, and skins are affected both by the characteristics of the variety and the degree of ripening. This is the reason why "good polyphenols" are sought as these give the wines a dense structure without the aggressiveness of "bad tannins", which are characterised by vegetal tastes and a herbaceous roughness in the mouth.

Another feature of red wine production is malolactic acid correction, which is better known as malolactic fermentation or secondary fermentation.

The classic stages are as follows:
- Treating the harvest: destemming, juice extraction and vatting.
- Alcoholic fermentation and maceration of the skins.
- Separating the wine from the pips and skins by racking and pressing.
- Malolactic acid correction.

On arrival at the bodega, the grapes are weighed and samples are collected for immediate analysis.

In our companies, the grapes are transported to the bodegas in crates containing between 20 kg (Áster, Torre de Oña and some of the La Rioja Alta, S.A. estates) and 350 kg (the remaining estates) so as to prevent damage or crushing. The usual practice locally is to transport the harvest in small trailers and move it from vineyard to bodega in the shortest possible time so as to avoid oxidation of the grapes. Refrigerated lorries are used to transport the harvest from the estates to the bodegas, with the result that the grapes arrive at the bodegas at a temperature of between 12° and 14°C. They are then kept at below 16°C during the first few days of alcoholic fermentation, thereby avoiding some of the dangers of the fermentation process (such as production of volatile acidity, fermentation halts) and the emergence of undesirable aromas and tastes.

Another advantage of this approach is that it enables pre-fermentation cold maceration, a technique which involves carrying out part of the maceration of the skins in the must, with the aim of maximising the extraction of aromas and colour, thereby boosting the terroir effect of each area. It is no coincidence that this technique originated in the French region of Burgundy, the promised land of terroir wines, from whence it spread to California and then throughout the rest of the world. This technique, known in English as either cold soaking or cold soak, chills the harvest down to 4-7°C, at which temperature it is then kept for some 7 to 10 days prior to fermentation. At La Rioja Alta, S.A., this technique has been implemented since the 2008 harvest.

Once the fruit has arrived at the bodega, each batch is weighed and samples are collected for qualitative analysis. In Áster and Torre de Oña, where the harvest is transported in crates, the bunches are spread out on a selection table where those in poor condition are removed, as are the leaves and loose vine stalks. The grapes are then moved on to the de-stalking, where the stalks are removed from the grape berries, with the top quality grapes then going to the juice extractors and the inferior grapes being removed.

The pulp from the harvest is pumped through into the fermentation vats, which are filled from the top and up to a maximum of 80% of their capacity, so that there is room to accommodate the increase in volume which fermentation produces. After three or four hours, the solid parts of the grapes form a layer on top of the must, known as a cap or "sombrero", while the heavier seeds sink to the bottom of the vats.

ALCOHOLIC FERMENTATION AND MACERATION OF THE SKINS

This is one of the most critical stages of the vinification process. Alcoholic fermentation varies according to the characteristics of the harvest and the temperature of the pulp when it is pumped into the vats. Hot years are associated with early harvests, sugar-rich musts, low acidity and likely problems in completing fermentation and it is, therefore, advisable to refrigerate the harvest to about 16°C before starting the fermentation process with a pre-prepared culture from the bottom of another barrel. This has been prepared by filling a small vat with 2,000 to 3,000 kilos of grapes and adding yeast to force fermentation. Once fermentation is fully under way, the contents are put into another vat which has recently been filled with grape must, thereby adding a significant quantity of yeasts to the second vat so as to trigger the fermentation process. This procedure is then repeated for all of the vats. There are currently available on the market a number of Dry Active Yeasts which can be rehydrated and then used as starter yeasts for the fermentation process. In complete contrast in cold areas or years, where the temperature of the must may be as low as 10°C, the crop must be warmed to 20°C before fermentation can begin. It starts slowly and releases a small amount of carbon dioxide which is easy to detect as it extinguishes the flame of a lighter or a candle held near the mouth of the vat. Furthermore, the temperature inside the vat increases progressively. After two or three days, a turbulent phase begins when large quantities of carbon dioxide are released which then bubble up in the vats, creating foam on the surface of the cap and a sudden increase in temperature. Fermentation in our bodegas is carried out at between 25° and 28°C, a temperature range which encourages the fermentation process and facilitates maceration of the skins to the level required for the style of wine to be produced. The must is monitored and checked daily through density and temperature measurements. The density of must is higher than that of wine and, as fermentation progresses, the density level drops from its initial value until it is below 1.000 g/l. The daily data are used to prepare graphs which show the fermentation dynamics and make it possible to see any changes during the process (halts and/or slowing down).

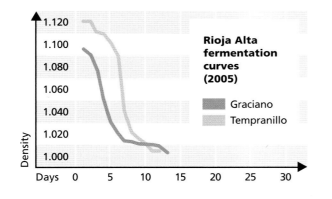

At La Rioja Alta, S.A., alcoholic fermentation is monitored using electrochemical sensors which measure the fermentation dynamics, providing real time data about the course of the fermentation process.

Once the wine is deemed dry, i.e. with no sugar left, it is tasted and analyses are carried out to establish the alcohol content, the fixed acidity, polyphenol levels and the other parameters which determine a wine's quality.

FERMENTATIVE MACERATION OF THE SKINS

Once in the vat, the grape skins form a cap, known as a sombrero. Maceration involves extracting the noble compounds from the skins (tannins, anthocyanins and aromas) in order to transfer and fix them in the must/wine and there are various mechanisms which make this process easier. At La Rioja Alta, S.A., remontage is the preferred method and involves removing part of the must from the bottom of the vat and moving it to the upper part where, using a spraying system similar to a shower, the must/wine is sprayed over the entire surface of the cap and creates cracks through which it passes, extracting the above mentioned compounds as it does so. Another way to do this is to use a mechanical system situated in the

The quality control manager analyses various parameters using a spectrophotometer to grade a batch of grapes. ∼∂ Once in the vat, the remontage extracts the colour from the skins, and transfers it to the must.

After pressing, the container is emptied and the skins are sent for distillation. At Lagar de Cervera, they are used as a base and are mixed with Albariño wine to make Viña Armenteira aguardiente.

upper part of the vat which cracks and breaks up the cap, producing a similar result. This system is known as head plunging, or cap immersion. A third method is "delastage" which is widely used in Côte de Rhône and involves emptying all of the must/wine out of the tank and then, some hours later, putting it back in; with the final effect being similar to that produced with head plunging.

The timing of maceration is critical for correct extraction. If the container is emptied too early, part of the richness of the grapes stays in the skin whilst, inversely, if left too long excessive extraction takes place and the wine become astringent, harsh, bitter and herbaceous.

The decision on maceration timing has to take into account the type of wine, the health of the grapes and the degree of phenol ripeness. If the objective is to produce young wines, the maceration time needs to be relatively short, aiming for a balanced extraction of colour and fruity aromas. A maceration period of a few days will generally be adequate. Maceration times for La Rioja Alta, S.A. wines are slightly longer, boosting extraction of colour and tannin so as to give the wine the structure required in light of its ultimate destination, as a Crianza, a Reserva or a Gran Reserva. Clearly, if the health of the grapes is poor, then it is inadvisable to prolong maceration.

RIOJA TEMPRANILLO, 2005 HARVEST	AT EMPTYING	AT PRESSING
Alcohol content (%)	12.9	12.0
Reductant sugars (g/l)	1.90	2.60
Dry extract (g/l)	24.20	29.30
Total acidity (g/l)	4.90	5.30
Volatile acidity (g/l)	0.35	0.45
Anthocyanins (mg/l)	330	400
Tannins (g/l)	1.75	3.20

SEPARATING THE WINE FROM THE SKINS AND PIPS USING RACKING AND PRESSING

Alcoholic fermentation ends when all the sugars in the must are used up, whereas the end point of maceration is a technical decision. Emptying the vat involves decanting the wine produced into a new container, in which malolactic fermentation will take place, and collecting the skins in the wine so that they can then be pressed. Pressed wine constitutes 15% of the total output, although this percentage may vary depending on the size of the grapes. The fermented and pressed dry skins are known as the "marc".

The pressed wine has a lower alcohol content, higher volatile acidity, higher concentration of reductant sugars and, significantly, a greater concentration of tannins, than the free-run wine.

MALOLACTIC ACID CORRECTION

TINTO DEL PAIS (RIBERA DE DUERO, 2005)	CONTROL WINE	MALOLACTIC (VAT)	MALOLACTIC (BARREL)
Alcohol content (%)	14.2	14.1	14.0
Total Acidity (g/l)	5.80	5.07	5.12
pH	3.68	3.73	3.72
Volatile Acidity (g/l)	0.31	0.49	0.55
Malic acid (g/l)	1.79	0.15	0.40
Lactic acid	0.10	1.34	1.15
Colour intensity	22.40	18.96	19.63
TPI (Total Polyphenol Index)	72	68	67

Wine ageing in barrels. Racking is carried out every six months at La Rioja Alta, S.A., except in the final years of Gran Reservas, when racking is carried out less frequently so as to maintain the fruit and freshness.

Although vinification is an ancient practice, malolactic fermentation was not studied in depth until 1961 when Jean Ribéreau-Gayon and Émile Peynaud carried out their research. It is a relatively simple phenomenon and is, in the case of fine red wines, a determinant factor of quality. Once the wines have been emptied out of the vats, a gentle bubbling can be seen in the sediments which is produced by the CO_2 released during the process of conversion.

The results of this process are analysed and, once all the malic acid has been converted into lactic acid, the wine is decanted into a new container where it will remain undisturbed as it completes the vinification process. If it is to be drunk as young wine then it will be bottled or else it will be put into barrel to age.

Although the conversion usually takes place in large concrete or stainless steel vats, there is one exception which is widespread in the white and red wines of Burgundy, namely malolactic fermentation in barrel. In this instance, once the alcoholic fermentation is at an end, the wine is transferred into barrels and the lees are stirred (batônnage) while this second conversion is ongoing, so that the yeast crusts come into contact with the wine. Wines produced using this technique have a more stable colour and better length.

At La Rioja Alta, S.A., malolactic fermentation is carried out in stainless steel vats, while at the Áster and Torre de Oña estates it is carried out in new barrels of French and American oak.

CARBONIC MACERATION

This technique is very widely used in the Rioja Alavesa and Rioja Alta regions. Wines made using carbonic maceration are characterised by their delicacy, light body and smoothness in the mouth, with their main appeal being in their characteristic aromas which are fresh and fruity. Carbonic maceration tends to be best suited to new wines which are to be drunk young or "en primeur" and there has been much controversy about its possible application in wines to be aged in barrels.

The technique involves two stages:

DURING THE FIRST STAGE, the grapes harvested into 20 kg crates are transported to the bodega in a manner which leaves the grapes as undamaged as possible. The bunches are weighed and then emptied into the vat, or "lake" intact, i.e. not destemmed or pressed and with great care being taken not to damage them or lose any of the must. The grapes are kept there for between 8 and 15 days and it is during this stage that the grapes begin to undergo the anaerobic metabolic reactions of carbonic maceration. The berries split and the coloured must emerges and starts to ferment. The length of this stage varies, depending on the wines being produced and the temperature at which it is taking place. For example at a temperature of 32°C it will last between 5 and 8 days, whereas at 15°C it will last between 15 and 20 days.

DURING THE SECOND STAGE, the vat is emptied and the marc is pressed. Initially the strained wine, which is a highly coloured must/wine known as free run wine, is taken out and then the rest of the harvest (complete bunches, undamaged berries, skin, etc.) is removed; this will later become the press wine.

Traditionally, devatting was done by people climbing into the vats and treading the harvest, with the must/wine draining out of the bottom bit by bit and the solid residue being taken out of the top to go for pressing. Once these two types of wine were devatted, they were then mixed so as to enable alcoholic fermentation to take place over a period of 5 days at a temperature of 20°C. Although this is a technique which is used to produce fine red wines, it has also been used to produce rosés and sweet aromatised wines.

PRODUCTION OF WHITE WINES
(FOR EXAMPLE LAGAR DE CERVERA)

White wines are made using white grape must or uncoloured pulp from red grapes. Must extraction and its clarification therefore precede alcoholic fermentation in this method of production. White wines with a residual sugar concentration below 2 g/l are known as "dry", although they can be produced with higher sugar levels, in which case they are given different names.

	SUGAR (G/L)
Dry	Below 5
Off dry	Between 5 and 15
Medium dry	Between 15 and 30
Medium sweet	Between 30 and 50
Sweet	Above 50

At Lagar de Fornelos, efforts are being made to increase the varietal aroma in dry white wine. Nevertheless, this is not all there is to a Rias Baixas white wine – refinement, complexity, the balance between the acid and sweet tastes, the feeling of body, of structure and of length in the mouth, all play a very important part in the final quality of a Lagar de Cervera wine. In order to achieve all of these attributes, we need to use healthy and ripe grapes from our own vineyards in a painstaking production process.

MUST EXTRACTION

During the various stages prior to fermentation it is important to avoid any oxidation or maceration of the must which can give the wine a vegetal and herbaceous character. The grapes are collected in 20 kg crates and then transported to the bodega in refrigerated lorries. The crates are emptied directly into the hopper where the bunches are destemmed. The harvest, with the grapes still intact, is then transferred to the presses where the must is produced, with this representing approximately 65% of the weight of the grapes. The unfermented skins are kept in small, sealed barrels and will be distilled after fermentation. These distillates will then be used to make dry and aromatic aguardientes, such as Viña Armenteira which is produced by Lagar de Fornelos, S.A. In certain regions, such as Champagne, the grapes are transferred directly to the presses without first being destemmed or compressed and before maceration of the skin must can really get underway, making it possible to achieve white musts from red grapes such as the Pinot Noir.

DEBOURBAGE

The freshly pressed must contains particles from the grapes in suspension and it is advisable to remove these so as to reduce the risk of oxidation or any vegetal character occurring and to increase the varietal aromas. In order to do this, the must is put into special containers in which it is stored at low temperatures (between 5° C and 10°C) for 24 to 48 hours, thereby avoiding triggering fermentation. During this time large particles drop to the bottom of the vat, leaving the supernatant wine clean and ready to be fermented. The residue, known as lees, is removed and can be used to obtain distillates once it has been fermented.

ALCOHOLIC FERMENTATION

Once the residue has been removed, the must is prepared for fermentation and transferred to a fresh vat. The must contains very low levels of yeasts and nutrients and it is, therefore, necessary to add these in advance, either by adding fermenting must from another barrel or by adding dry yeasts which will trigger fermentation. This is carried out at temperatures below 20°C, so as to conserve the varietal aromas, and ordinarily the process lasts for between 15 and 20 days, during which time the sugar levels drop to below 2 g/l. At Lagar de Fornelos, partial malolactic fermentation is also carried out in stainless steel vats, with the degree to which this is done depending on the characteristics of the harvest. Although it is a process which to some extent lessens the varietal character of Albariño, it also improves the complexity and gives a greater structure in the mouth, when carried out in a controlled manner.

Finally, the wines are transferred and stored in stainless steel vats until they are ready for bottling. It is important during this phase to monitor the temperature in the vat area, ensuring that the temperatures remain low enough to inhibit any unwanted microbiological growth.

In Burgundy, wines from the Chardonnay grape are traditionally produced in 228 litre oak barrels. In this instance, the residue is removed from the must which is then put into oak barrels which already contain wine; thereafter the must is fermented at between 16° and 18°C. Once fermentation is finished, the barrels are refilled with wine from the same batch and the lees are stirred manually (batônnage) each day; malolactic fermentation may or may not then take place. The wine then remains in barrel for three to four months during which time it becomes impregnated with elements of the wood which improves the structure and smoothness in the mouth and gives it a special character.

PRODUCTION OF ROSE WINES

A rosé wine comes either from a red grape or a mixture of red and white grapes, where the must was fermented without the skins. Rosé wines are fermented in the same way as white wines and owe their colour to a light maceration which is completed before the start of fermentation and can be of variable duration. Rosés are, therefore, produced in the same way as white wines. Top quality rosé wines are usually made with red varieties which are not well suited to ageing and are, generally, monovarietal. Fine Spanish examples are Garnacha in Navarra and Cariñena, and in France with the Gamay grape, Beaujolais being a good example.

The term "clarete" is used for those wines which are made from musts comprising a mixture of white and red grapes where the must has undergone a light maceration with the skins during the fermentation process. They are made in the same way as red wines and the best known are the wines of Valdepeñas (made with a must comprising some 80% white Airen grapes and 20% Tempranillo grapes) and from Rioja the wines of Badarán and Cordovín (made with a similar ratio of Viura and Garnacha).

OTHER TYPES OF PRODUCTION

In addition to the fundamental processes involved in the three most common types of production (red, white and rosé) there are other production methods, generally confined to a specific product or particular region. Some of these produce very special wines, having great personality and originality and being found nowhere else in the world. The following wines stand out:

CHAMPAGNES AND CAVAS are wines in which the bubbles form during a secondary fermentation phase in the bottle.

SHERRIES are finos and olorosos, with added alcohol and given personality by the famous flor.

SAUTERNES AND DESSERT WINES are sweet wines produced from grapes infected with the Botrytis cinerea fungus which, once inside the grape berry, causes water evaporation which in turn increases the concentration of the elements which make up the juice.

THE SPLENDID WINES OF OPORTO have an alcohol content of between 4-5 degrees to which brandy is added in order to stop fermentation, thereby producing a sweet wine with a final alcohol level of some 20 degrees which is then stored over a number of years in barrel or bottle.

THE WINES OF TOKAJI are made in Hungary from grapes infected with botrytis.

ICE WINES (EISWEIN) are made primarily in Germany, Austria, Switzerland and Canada, with musts from the pressing of late, healthy harvests which had been frozen by the winter frosts.

ECOLOGICAL AND BIODYNAMIC WINES are made from grapes cultivated using ecological, biodynamic or biological methods, which aim to produce better quality products by using techniques which respect the environment and preserve the fertility of the land, using natural resources to the greatest possible extent without recourse to any form of chemical intervention.

The cooperage, with its artisanship and traditions, the beauty of its tools and its fittings, is home to an art which has been practised at La Rioja Alta, S.A., since it was founded.

OAK

The raw staves from the United States are stacked so as to allow the air to circulate freely to dry out the wood. After some two years exposed to the elements the wood is ready to be made into barrels.

ak is the main element in the ageing of a wine and its possibilities are vast. Not all barrels are the same and wines will evolve in different ways depending on the origin of the wood, the extent to which the wood is toasted, the quality of the grape, etc. This section will look briefly at the history of oak, its components and origins, and how it is made into barrels.

HISTORY AND BACKGROUND TO BARREL AGEING

The use of oak barrels in ageing wines has its origins in a historic need to transport the wines from the rural regions where they were produced to the areas where they were being drunk, usually towns and cities, by a population with a greater purchasing power. The first data relating to the use of wood for transporting wine dates from Roman times, in the northern areas of Europe where receptacles made of wood were used to store and transport beer and wine. There are few references to its use during the Middle Ages, except for mention of it being used in the monasteries and abbeys in Christian-dominated areas.

Oak was first used in France at the beginning of the 14th century when it was used to transport wine from the lands of Burgundy to the Low Countries, Flanders and Holland, primarily along the Spanish Way, a route for moving troops between Italy, Flanders and Germany. During this period, oak barrels from Nevers, Allier and Vosges were used. At the start of the 16th century chestnut and cherry wood began to be used for barrels in the Iberian peninsula, primarily because there was widespread deforestation of Spanish oak groves as a result of the harvesting of wood for the raw material to construct the Spanish fleet, which had been decimated by the continuous wars in which it had been embroiled. During this period the cooperages of Cádiz and Jerez began to flourish, thanks to imports of American oak.

During the 16th and 17th centuries, the Bordelais used barrels made of oak from the nearby region of Limousin to transport their wines to Paris and the emerging English market. As with wines from other regions such as Oporto, Madeira and Jerez, the journey to England took some two to three weeks by sea and the wine travelled in wooden containers, during which voyage it suffered various changes,

Our limited production volume means that each of our artisans must be capable of making an entire barrel, and each of the individual parts, which helps us to keep alive the demanding art of the cooper.

some of which were not pleasant. This led to the wine being topped-up with brandy so as to avoid it suffering these unpleasant changes during the journey and ensure that it arrived at its destination in good condition. At the start of the 18th century there was a recipe in Bordeaux for ensuring that wines arrived in England in good condition which was known as "travail à l'anglaise" and consisted of topping up each 225 litre barrel with 30 litres of wine from Alicante, 2 litres of white must and a bottle of brandy one to two years before the wine was due to travel.

Another important market for Bordeaux at this time were the Baltic States, primarily Prussia and Poland. French ships would set out with their cargos of wine and return with cargos of staves from the oak groves of Poland, Pomerania and Prussia. These woods were thought to be the best for producing barrels for high quality wines, because they imparted a less strong oak flavour and a more pleasant tannin one.

In 1661 an event took place in France which would be decisive in French forestry and the wine industry. Jean-Baptiste Colbert, a minister, launched a major replanting of French oak groves which had been badly depleted by the harvesting of wood for war ships; there was no equivalent reforestation programme in Spain. The replanting was managed by the State on an ongoing basis which meant that it was possible to harvest more than 3 million cubic metres of wood every year.

In Spain barrel ageing was introduced by Don Manuel Quintano in the 18th century in the bodegas of Labastida, although the next significant step was not taken until 1850 when Don Luciano de Murrieta introduced the modern production methods of Bordeaux, including barrel ageing. At that time Rioja wine makers did not use barrels and in order to accomplish the first trials in his new bodega he had to buy little kegs (a quarter of the size of a barrel) in Bilbao.

His experiments resulted in the hitherto rough and rude Rioja wines of the day becoming smoother and developing new and elegant flavours. At the same time, Don Camilo Hurtado de Amezaga, Marqués de Riscal, built an attractive bodega in Elciego-Álava in the style of a French château as part of his efforts to replicate the wines of Bordeaux. He also planted 202 hectares of Rioja varieties, primarily Tempranillo, and others from Bordeaux such as Cabernet Sauvignon. Using techniques imported from the Médoc, he stored his fine wines (Reservas) in barrels and then in Bordeaux bottles which were wrapped and sealed with a wire mesh. In 1865 a Marqués de Riscal Tempranillo wine was entered in a famous tasting in Bordeaux where it won the first prize and introduced top quality Spanish wines to the rest of the world. Over time, consumers' tastes have adapted to wines aged in barrels and the changes which take place in the barrel have been accepted as an essential stage in the process of producing quality wines. The problem which then arose was that wine cannot stay in barrels for an indefinite length of time otherwise it will turn into vinegar. The solution to this was to decant the wine into glass bottles with a cork stopper. Thus the "art and fashion of producing wine" assimilated the notion of a period of storage in wooden barrels or casks followed by a more or less permanent storage in bottle.

In the mid 20th century use of wooden containers fell out of fashion as the use of inert materials, such as reinforced concrete or stainless steel, became widespread. By the 1960s and 1970s the barrel

The oak woods of our supplier in Tennessee, where the majority of the staves which we use to make our barrels come from.

stores in the bodegas comprised mostly very old barrels in very poor condition. It was not until the 1980s and 1990s, that research driven by the wine and cooperage industries, led to a significant reintroduction of barrels in virtually all Rioja bodegas. Existing barrels had to be refurbished and at the same time new oaks from different regions were introduced, as were different levels of toasting and new sealing systems (silicon stoppers etc). During this period there was both a boom in new wine producing countries, primarily Australia, Chile, the United States (California) and South Africa, and new materials which "replaced" the flavours and aromas achieved through barrel ageing. The most well-known are oak shavings, chips or planks.

OAK

Oak belongs to the genus *Quercus*, family *Fagaceae*, subfamily *Quercoideae*. More than 600 species are grown in Europe, North America and South America. In Europe there are some 29 different species but only two are used in cooperage, namely *Quercus petraea* or *sessilis* and *Quercus robur* or *pedunculata*. France is the main grower of these two species. *Quercus petraea* is grown primarily in Central France (Allier, Tronçais and Nevers) and in the Burgundy, Vosges and Argonne regions, using the *haute futaie* (high planting) technique and producing tall, high quality trees.

Quercus robur grows primarily in the Limousin region and the south west of Aquitaine. It is grown using the *taillis sous futaie* (low planting) technique which requires a great deal of light and fertile soils.

In Spain the two species are grown together with no regional distinctions, primarily in the north and north-east of the Iberian peninsula. *Quercus Pyrenaica* is also grown and is known as the Pyrenean oak or Turkey oak but it is not used in cooperage. In America some 24 species are grown, but only *Quercus Alba* (known in the USA as *True White Oak*) is used in barrel making. It grows on the East Coast of the USA, with the states of Missouri, Ohio, Illinois, Tennessee and Kentucky being the main production areas.

In order to produce high quality wood, the trees must have forest stature, i.e. great height, single and erect trunk, crown limited to a third or half of the tree's height and a cylindrical trunk of significant diameter. The *haute futaie* technique produces better quality trees for making barrels.

TYPES AND STRUCTURE

A transverse section of a trunk shows the different layers of which it is comprised. From the outside inwards, the first layer is made up of *bark* which protects the wood after which there is another living internal bark. Next, there is a layer known as the cambium which determines the tree's width and which covers a pale layer known as *sapwood*, which is responsible for conducting sap and storing nutrients. The *heartwood* is the next layer and is a dark and very thick layer made up of dead cells

Each barrel is like a piece of furniture and creating it demands the same meticulousness and care.

Heartwood   Sapwood   Pith   Cambium   Internal bark   External bark

and responsible for supporting the tree. Lastly, there is the *pith* which is soft tissue surrounded by the initial outward growth of the stem.

The rings of growth are formed by the activity of the cambium which causes the trunk to grow thicker each year, forming new wood internally and bark externally. The rate of growth establishes the width of the ring and is determined by the species and the location and the conditions in which the tree is growing. The width of the ring is known as the grain of the wood and this is described as fine where the rate of growth has been slow and coarse where it has been more rapid. A cooper needs to work with strong woods which are porous and permeable enough and such criteria are met where a wood has rings of a certain width and a smooth texture.

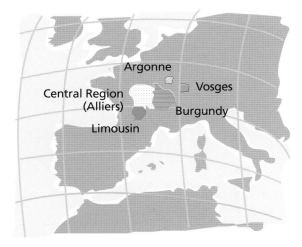

THE OAK FORESTS OF FRANCE

CHEMICAL COMPOSITION OF OAK WOOD

It is made up of 40% cellulose, 25% lignin, about 20% hemicelluloses, some 10% ellagitannins and about 5% of other compounds. The first three provide the mechanical characteristics of tensile and compression strength, give the structure rigidity and form the skeleton of the wood. The remaining components form the removable sub-section and contribute to the other properties of the wood, such as the colour, flavour and resistance to decay. Ellagitannins are extremely important in the ageing of wines since they have antioxidant qualities, promote anthocyanin condensation and contribute to the bitterness and astringency of a wine. The quantity of ellagitannins falls as the wood is dried naturally in the open air and then toasted during the making of a barrel.

Other chemical compounds found in wood which may be transferred to a wine include low molecular weight polyphenols (vanillin), volatile compounds (furfural), lactones, phenols (eugenol), ketones, etc.

La Rioja Alta, S.A. imports American oak from Ohio, Missouri, Tennessee and Kentucky and then leaves it to dry naturally at Labastida for a minimum of two years. At present between 4,000 and 5,000 barrels are made each year in our own cooperage and are then used to keep our barrel stock replenished.

along the banks of rivers, is used to wrap the stoppers for the esquive at the front of the barrel. The esquive can also hold the tap used for racking the wine.

The geographic origin of oak, together with its botanical species, has a considerable influence on the characteristics which will be imparted to the wine during barrel ageing. AMERICAN OAK characteristically imparts volatile compounds, such as methyl-octalactones, which give aromas of coconut, vanillin, guaiacol (aroma of toasted caramel) or eugenol (aroma of cloves). However, they are woods which impart few tannins to the wines and they therefore contribute little to its tannicity. The wines of La Rioja Alta, S.A., have a characteristic and very well-defined aroma profile, with the typical aromas of the grape combining with the spicy and balsamic aromas of American oak. This kind of oak ensures the subtlety and elegance of the wines without making them hard.

With regard to FRENCH OAK, a distinction must be drawn between the different botanical species. *Quercus robur*, which is grown primarily in Limousin, typically has low aroma intensity, with only a slight input of vanillin and coconut but a substantial ellagic tannin contribution which help strengthen and toughen the structure of the wines. In contrast, French oak of the *Quercus petraea* species, which is cultivated in the Allier region, makes a significant aroma contribution, albeit less so than that of American oak. It does, however, bring a more complex aroma profile, which is balanced and elegant by virtue of being less marked by vanillin and coconut, and it introduces an important nuance of cloves. With regard to tannins, it makes a small contribution to the structure of the wine. Furthermore, French oak is very influenced by the size and uniformity of the grain.

Regardless of the species of oak, those with a fine grain bring great aromatic richness to the wine and strengthen it only to a slight degree whereas coarse grain oaks yield the opposite result, i.e. they increase the sturdiness of the wine but have only a slight impact on its aroma. For all of the above reasons, fine grained oaks are considered to be of better quality for making wines with a clear *terroir* effect.

In Torre de Oña, S.A. and Áster, where the wines produced use grapes only from our own vineyards, barrels made of fine grained French oak from Allier are used and these give a light structure to the wines and enable the varietal aromas of the grapes from these most special lands to be retained.

With regard to CENTRAL EUROPEAN OAKS (predominantly from Hungary, Poland and the Caucasus Mountains), in terms of their characteristics they are somewhere in between American oak and oak from Allier. They typically impart smooth tannins and yield very "sweet" wines with a medium aroma profile. We have found this to be a type of oak which adapts in an interesting way to the Tempranillo wines of the Rioja Alavesa region, by slightly increasing the structure and the varietal complexity of the Tempranillo grapes from the Páganos vineyard and, on the basis of this, a research project is being carried out into the use of Caucasian oak in Torre de Oña.

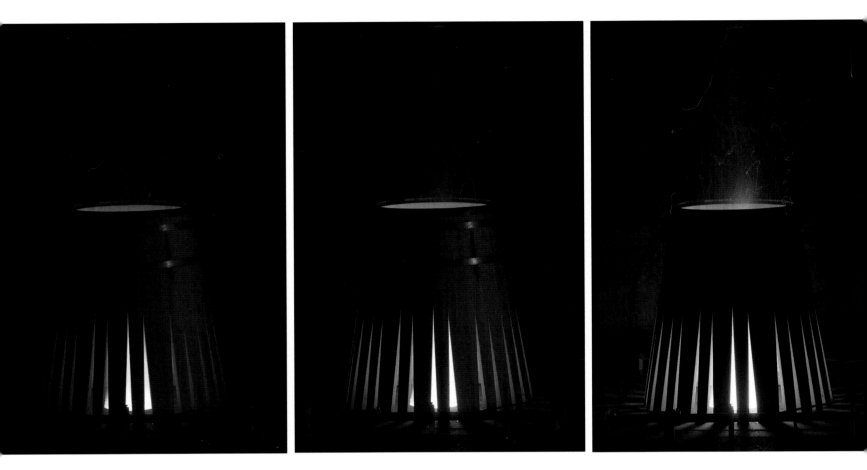

BARREL MAKING

SELECTING THE TREES AND OBTAINING THE STAVES. This is a two stage process. Between September and November the trees are selected on the basis of their external appearance for felling in each of the regions and they are then felled between November and February. Once felled, the trees are selected as a function of their different qualities in terms of height, the breadth of the trunk and the absence of knots, wounds or any rottenness. Wood destined for cooperage must come from the lower part of the trunk, i.e. the part with no branches, with the remainder going for cabinet making and the construction industry. These trunks are then cut into pieces of suitable length, from which the bark and sapwood is removed, because only the heartwood has the necessary properties for barrel production. The pieces are then divided up into dressed timber planks, from which the staves are cut. There are two methods of producing the staves, by saw-cutting, which is used for American oak and has a higher yield (some 3.7 barrels per m³ of wood) or by splitting which is used with European oaks which, by virtue of their porosity and permeability, do not guarantee water tightness and must therefore be cut in parallel with the medullar radii.

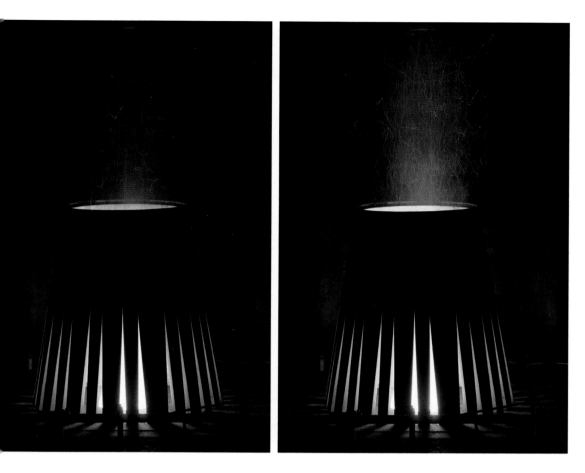

The yield from splitting is lower (2.2 barrels per m³ of wood) and this is probably the main reason why French oak barrels are more expensive than American oak ones.

DRYING. The staves are between 22mm and 30mm thick and, with a water content of between 35% and 60%, must undergo a drying process. Natural drying is the ideal, with the staves being seasoned in the open air for two to three years until the wood humidity is between 15% and 17%. During this period, the wood goes through distinct phases of hydration/dehydration as a result of rains or artificial watering and the heat of the sun, all of which contribute to the slow and comprehensive curing of the wood which is transformed from a green and vigorous wood to a drier and more aromatic one, losing bitterness and astringency which are undesirable qualities in wines. The drying process can also be carried out in drying chambers which will accelerate the process by increasing the temperature and rate of ventilation although, as with any artificial acceleration process, it does not produce the same quality of wood.

ASSEMBLY AND TOASTING. Once the staves have been dried, they are fitted together into circular structures which are held in place by metal hoops, with the aim of assembling them into barrels. In order to temper the staves and form them into the characteristic shape of a barrel they are heated

177

over a fire, a process known as toasting. Heating the staves enables them to be bent using the mechanical action of a winch. This process is called tempering the staves or shape toasting. One important aspect to point out is that the stave humidity level after the drying phase must be appropriate, because if the humidity level is too low, there is the risk that the staves will split during the shaping process. On the other hand, if the internal humidity level of the wood is too high, then blisters will form on the surface of the wood which will encourage leaks and steeping of the wine into the wood, which may later cause changes. When the wood comes into contact with the fire, a series of chemical changes is triggered which affects the combination of the substances which the barrel may impart to the wine during ageing. The length of time the wood is in contact with the fire determines whether these changes will be great or small and it, therefore, has a considerable influence on the chemical and sensory impact that the wood will have on the wine. Where toasting is carried out after the barrel is assembled, it is known as finishing toasting which can be classified according to duration as light, medium or strong. It must be borne in mind that each cooperage or bodega will have its own toasting protocol and that the criteria may, therefore, be different. Furthermore, some manufacturers specify different levels of medium toasting, differentiating between medium plus toasting, medium low toasting and extra strong toasting. The source of the heat for toasting may be small braziers containing oak cut-offs, with the temperature being monitored using laser beams. In order to toast the bottom of a barrel, electrical resistance is used to control the heat being applied.

Once all of these processes are complete, the barrel is at last ready for the final assembly stage which comprises switching the initial assembly hoops for other, lighter hoops, the bottom being inserted, the surface being sanded and water tightness and overall appearance being checked. All of this requires a highly qualified and experienced workforce. In modern, industrial cooperages each operation is broken down into specialised tasks but in the more traditional bodegas the cooper must be skilled in each of the steps involved in making a barrel. It is a long and expensive apprenticeship with the result that there are nowadays very few master coopers. This dearth of such specialised artisans is all the more painful in terms of the production of the wooden vats, tubs and barrels used for fermentation and maceration of wines. The number of master coopers in Spain can be counted on the fingers of one hand but at least there are some.

THE LEVEL OF TOASTING OF A BARREL GREATLY INFLUENCES THE AROMAS IN THE WINE

Bilge Bung hole Master stave Bilge hoop Quarter hoop Chime hoop Chime Chime

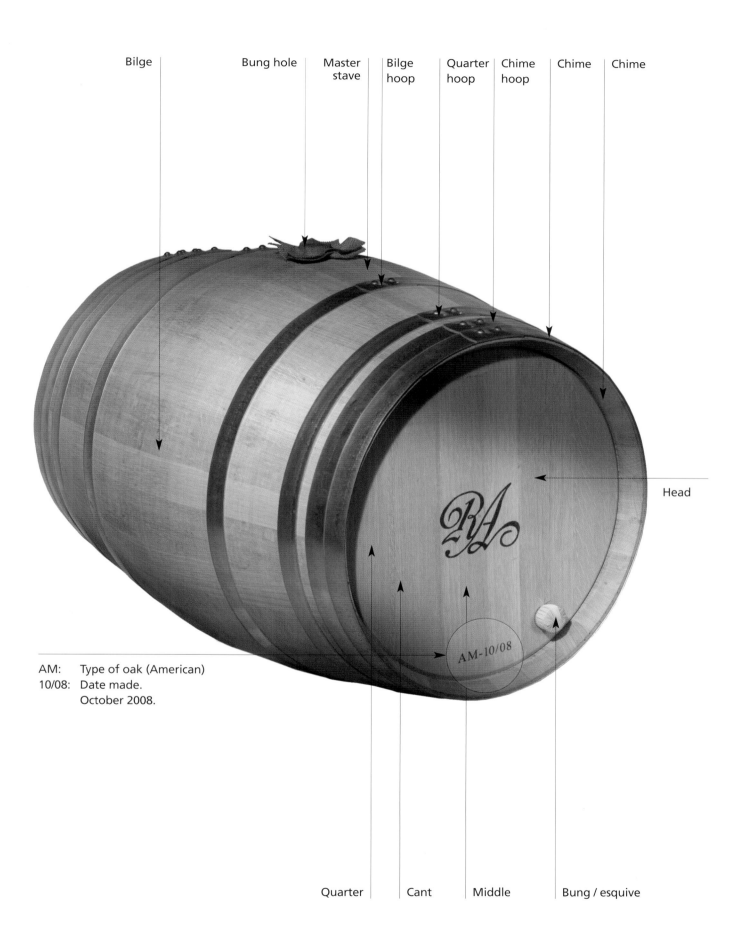

Head

AM: Type of oak (American)
10/08: Date made.
October 2008.

Quarter Cant Middle Bung / esquive

The Experimental Room at La Rioja Alta, S.A., where different varieties, coupages, types of oak, number of decantings, ageing etc. are all investigated.

BARREL
AGEING

Racking by gravity, barrel to barrel, enables the wine to be oxygenated, each barrel to be monitored individually and sediments to be removed, without the need to use pumps or other machinery.

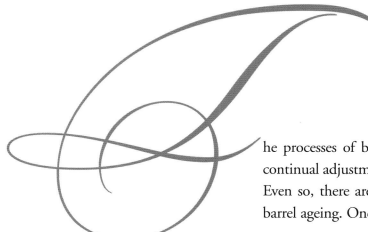

he processes of barrel ageing are varied, require complex monitoring and continual adjustments by the oenologists, to define the wine to be produced. Even so, there are alternative techniques which claim to be substitutes for barrel ageing. One wonders, however, whether that is really possible.

THE PROCESSES WHICH TAKE PLACE

The main reason that wine is aged in oak is that it imparts aromas and phenolic compounds which improve its aromatic and taste qualities. There are, however, other very positive reasons. Barrel ageing allows for a moderate degree of oxygenation by virtue of the porosity of the wood, through the stave joins and the esquive. This process of natural micro-oxygenation provides the substratum necessary to trigger the reactions which polymerise and blend the anthocyanins and tannins. This leads to the colour becoming stable and smoothing of the astringency. There is also some precipitation of the colouring agents in the wine, clearly the more unstable part, which means that the precipitate does not then later appear in the bottled wine.

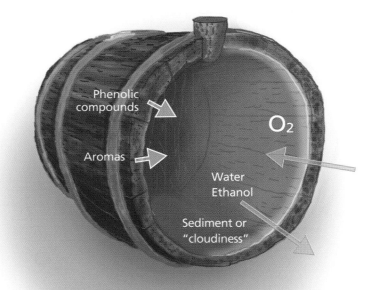

The imparting of aromas through barrel ageing depends on many factors, important among which are, as seen in the last chapter, the botanical and geographical origin of the oak, its grain, the drying process, the level of stave toasting and the age of the barrel. Some of the molecules which are responsible for the characteristic aromas from ageing are found naturally in the oak wood whilst others result from the drying and toasting of the staves.

The table below shows the different volatile substances which the oak imparts to a wine, from an organoleptic point of view.

VOLATILE COMPOUNDS		DESCRIPTION	ORIGIN
Furans	Furfural	Toasted almonds	Polysaccharides
	Methylfurfural		
	Hydroxymethylfurfural		
	Furfural alcohol		
Phenolic aldehydes	Maltol	Caramel, toast	
	Dimethyl pirazines	Coffee, toasted hazelnuts	
Acetic acid		Vinegar	
Coniferaldehyde	Vanillin	Vanilla	Lignins
	Syringaldehyde	–	
	Sinapaldehyde	–	
	Coniferaldehyde	–	
Phenyl ketones	Acetophenone	Vanilla	
	Acetovanillone		
	Propiovanillone		
	Butyrovanillone		
Volatile phenols	Guaiacol	Burnt	
	Methyl guaiacol		
	Ethylguaiacol		
	Eugenol	Cloves	
	4-ethyl-phenol	Sweaty saddles	
ß-Methyl γ-octalactone	cis isomer	Walnut, coconut, oak	Lipids
	trans isomer		

A significant negative aspect which must be stressed is that the longer the wine spends in the bodega and particularly in the barrel, the greater the likelihood of problems with quality, such as oxidation, vinegarisation, loss of colour, etc. Furthermore, storing the wines in barrels leads to evaporation of water and alcohol which causes loss and makes the process more expensive. There are, however, other problems. Toasting the staves creates acetic acid which may cause a not insignificant increase in the volatile acidity of ageing wines, particularly with new barrels, with the levels potentially reaching 0.15 g/l per annum. Nevertheless, the main source of acetic acid in wine (what is commonly referred to as "vinegarising") is never the wood but is by and large of microbiological origin and is attributable to acetic bacteria and possibly to lactic bacteria.

There are two other families of volatile substances which originate in oak and which are important, namely phenolic aldehydes and phenyl ketones. Vanillin stands out among the phenolic aldehydes on account of its importance to the senses, being the substance which is primarily responsible for the smell of vanilla which characterises many aged wines. Phenyl ketones also contribute to the aromas of aged wines and also impart a vanilla smell. The chemical origin of vanillin and the other aldehydes and ketones is to be found in lignin.

Volatile phenols are part of a large family of compounds found in oak and also contribute to the aroma of a wine. Guaiacol gives a toasted smell; 4-methyl guaiacol and 4-ethyl guaiacol the smell of burnt wood; 4-vinyl guaiacol a smell reminiscent of carnations; phenol the smell of ink; eugenol, which is of great organoleptic importance, gives a smell of cloves; 4-vinyl phenol gives phenolic and pharmaceutical notes; lastly 4-ethyl phenol imparts a disagreeable smell of animal, leather or horse sweat. The presence of this last compound is considered to be highly detrimental to the quality of the wine once it passes the perception threshold (thought by some scientists to be around 500 mg/l) and it is closely connected to a microbiological change caused by the growth of a yeast of the genus Brettanomyces. This is commonly known as the "Brett aroma".

Lastly, methyl octalactones are also important in the aroma of aged wines and particularly in wines from La Rioja Alta, S.A. These lactones, which are commonly known as whiskey lactones, are the source of the coconut smell which is characteristic of aged wines.

As can be seen from the graph, LIGHT TOASTING has a major aromatic impact and is notable for coconut aromas (whiskey lactones); it does however impart a high level

INFLUENCE OF THE LEVEL OF STAVE TOASTING ON AROMATIC IMPACT

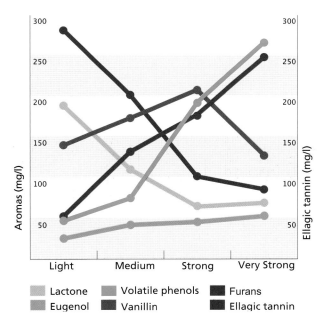

Potassium bitartrate crystals on barrel staves.

of ellagic tannin and, if the stave drying process was not long and thorough enough, it may impart excessive wood notes.

MEDIUM TOASTING results in a reduction in the overall aromatic impact compared with light toasting but yields gains in terms of balance and complexity. The coconut notes diminish and those of the other volatile substances increase, particularly vanillin. Furthermore, the ellagic tannin contribution is lower than is the case with light toasting.

STRONG TOASTING causes a slight loss in olfactory intensity but, more importantly, it affects enormously the balance between the families of aromas. It reduces fundamentally the coconut aromas and increases the volatile phenols, vanillin and furans. It also leads to a sharp drop in the ellagic tannins which the oak imparts to the wine.

Lastly, VERY STRONG TOASTING causes another slight drop in the overall intensity of the aroma and, above all, triggers a huge change with regard to the composition of the aromas. It causes a sharp rise in the volatile phenols and furans and a reduction in coconut and vanillin. The fall in the level of ellagic tannins directly correlates to the increase in the level of toasting.

In summary, it can be said that increasing the level of toasting reduces the coconut aromas and, logically, increases the notes of toast, spiciness and smokiness. The vanilla notes also increase as a function of toasting levels, albeit they fall with very strong toasting. Light toasting may impart excessive coconut and ellagic tannin aromas which can overly mark a wine. Medium toasting imparts a better balance between the notes of coconut, vanilla, toasting, spiciness and smokiness. Furthermore, the level of ellagic tannins which results from medium toasting can be considered the most suitable in terms of complementing the structure of the wine. Lastly, strong toasting may lead to excessive notes of smokiness and toasting which can give a wine too much of a dark-roasted character.

Nevertheless, as Chapter 10 will show, two very important factors are to be borne in mind when deciding the ideal level of toasting for barrels. On the one hand, there is the origin of the oak to consider, since its extractable compounds are influenced by its botanical and geographical origin and over-toasting may degrade these extractable compounds or alter their profile. Other factors to consider are the structure and type of wine which the barrels will hold.

THE PHYSICAL PROCESSES OF BARREL AGEING

As well as enriching the wine with substances which contribute to its sensory characteristics, barrels may also impart unwelcome properties if they are not properly cleaned and maintained. Good management of the ageing process entails diligent preparation and maintenance of the barrels, which differs depending on whether they are new or used.

NEW BARRELS. After the barrels are delivered, their physical condition is inspected (to check for breakages, the shape, appearance, type of oak and grain, etc.) and volume and water tightness are verified. After that, perhaps three barrels from a batch of fifty are selected, have their bottoms removed

Ageing area at Torre de Oña, S.A., with the Tasting Room in the background.
The Labastida bodega, with the barrels stacked five high.

and are examined internally, checking the toasting, that there are no strange smells and for blisters, etc. Before being filled they are washed by alternate cycles of hot water, steam and cold water. Once they are drained, sulphur lozenges (spills) are burned inside the barrels, unless malolactic fermentation in barrel is to be carried out, to ensure that they are hygienic, after which they are kept in a dry area until needed.

With USED BARRELS, a thorough cleaning and disinfection process is an absolute pre-requisite in order to be able to preserve them. After each racking, the barrels are thoroughly cleaned to eliminate as far as possible any lees or tartrates deposited on the inside. The subsequent washing process is similar to that previously described for new barrels. After the washing process, the barrels are then filled.

In order to ensure that the barrels remain in good condition, it is important to keep them filled with wine. If the barrels must be left empty for any time, they have to be carefully looked after by periodically washing and disinfecting them (once every 20 days) so as to safeguard both their physical condition (particularly given that drying the wood may lead to leaks developing) and their microbiological condition (growth of bacteria and yeasts of the genus Brettanomyces). Before using these barrels it is necessary to check their condition again, ruling out any with an unpleasant smell (rotten, Brett, etc.) or in poor condition.

ALTHOUGH NEW BARRELS MAY BE ADEQUATE FOR SHORT PERIODS OF AGEING, THEY ARE NOT USUALLY THE MOST SUITABLE FOR LONG AGEING CYCLES.

CONDITIONS IN THE AGEING AREA

During barrel ageing, wine suffers so-called "losses". These may result from absorption (the barrel is said to be drinking the wine) in which case their level depends on the state of the barrel but is higher when the barrel is new. Loss through evaporation is essentially governed by the temperature and the humidity of the premises. The ideal temperature is thought to be between 10°C and 15°C. Higher temperatures may cause the wine to develop more quickly and increase loss through evaporation. In contrast, lower temperatures may halt the development of the wine, although they do promote natural stabilisation by precipitating tartrates and volatile colouring agents. It is also advisable to protect against differences between the seasons of the year being too marked, so as to stop the wine expanding and/or contracting within the barrel. Expansion may lead to leakage from barrels whilst contraction may have the opposite effect, creating a significant void which will then require the barrel to be topped up; failure to do this may lead to the wine becoming sour.

The relative humidity of the barrel premises is another very important factor. It must be as high as possible so as to minimise loss through evaporation but not so high as to lead to condensation, as this may encourage fungi to grow in the ageing room or even on the surface of the barrels, with all the consequent risks of unpleasant mildew odours developing in the wine.

TEMPERATURE	RELATIVE HUMIDITY (%)					
	45%	55%	65%	75%	85%	95%
10°C	4.50	3.90	3.00	2.20	1.10	0.50
12°C	5.00	4.00	3.25	2.65	1.50	0.70
14°C	5.75	4.54	3.60	2.75	1.80	0.80
16°C	6.50	5.35	4.15	3.10	2.00	0.90
18°C	7.70	6.20	4.75	3.75	2.50	1.00

The above table shows the influence of temperature and humidity on wine loss through evaporation. As can be seen, at high temperatures and low relative humidity, the loss levels are very high at up to 7.7%. In contrast, loss levels are minimal at low temperatures and high relative humidity at just 0.5%.

It can be concluded that monitoring temperature and humidity in the ageing room is essential, not simply to ensure that the wine develops correctly but also to reduce loss which clearly affect economic yield. There are presently available on the market a variety of very efficient systems which enable the relative humidity to be increased, thereby reducing loss, as well as dehumidifiers which avoid any unwelcome condensation.

At La Rioja Alta, S.A., all the ageing premises in our bodegas which are not underground have been fitted with air conditioning and automatic humidification systems, as well as an automatic night-time air exchange system.

PREPARATION OF THE WINE

All wine which is intended to be aged in barrels has to meet certain advisable minimum conditions in terms of its chemical composition (alcohol level above 12%, balanced acidity, polyphenol levels above 50 on TPI, no fermentable sugars or malic acid, etc.). If wines which do not meet these criteria are aged, the resulting product is excessively oxidised and spoiled by the wood. One important aspect which conditions the future development of the wine during ageing is the process of preparing the wine for the barrels. At La Rioja Alta, S.A., the first step is the coupage of the wines which will make up each batch, which is followed by a gentle clarification process so that the wine going into the barrels is sufficiently clean. The barrels are filled using gravity and are then moved to the various stacks in the premises, where the process of ageing in wood begins. There are different types of ageing process, depending on the type of wine. We shall concentrate on the ageing of red wines.

The wine is channelled into the barrels, which have previously been prepared in the manner set out earlier. The most efficient way of moving wine is by gravity but this is not always possible, in which case it is necessary to use a small pump. It is advisable to control the final stages of the filling process by using a gun system at the end of the channelling run. Such a system makes it much easier to cut off the supply and avoid the wine overflowing. Unavoidable wine stains on the surface of the barrel can easily be cleaned off using a brush soaked in sulphited water. Once the barrel is full, the outer surface is gently hit with a rubber hammer so as to dislodge the bubbles which usually form on the inner surface of the barrel, so that the barrel can then filled up further. This process is known as topping up and must be repeated until the level of the wine stops falling. Sometimes barrels develop slight leaks which need to be sealed quickly with small wooden wedges, called plugs. Once the barrels are full, they are transferred to the ageing area to be stacked. Some bodegas stack barrels only one high, but in Rioja and Ribera del Duero the barrels are traditionally stacked either four or five high.

THE ROLE OF WINE RACKER, PASSED ON FROM FATHER TO SON, REQUIRES CARE, EXPERIENCE AND WISDOM.

RACKING BY HAND IS A FUNDAMENTAL STEP IN MONITORING QUALITY IN EACH BARREL.

The ageing process produces precipitates of tartrates and volatile colouring agents. Indeed one of the objectives of ageing is to stabilise the wine with respect to these precipitates and to clarify it naturally by decanting it. This is one of the reasons why the wine is decanted, by transferring it directly from one barrel to another, ideally by gravity, so as to eliminate so-called "cloudiness". Racking can be carried out either shielding the wine from the air or allowing a degree of aeration. In the case of a delicate wine, it is advisable to avoid oxygenation as far as possible whereas with a robust wine it can be advisable to aerate the wine during decanting in order to boost development of the colouring agents. Decanting with aeration can be also useful where reduction notes are detected in the wine.

Traditionally decanting was done directly from barrel to barrel. It is not a simple operation and requires co-operation between various craftsmen. The esquive (lower) bung is taken out of the initial barrel and immediately replaced with a stopcock or "tap". This operation has to be carried out with the greatest of care to avoid spilling the wine and it is essential to put a funnel immediately underneath to

catch any spillage. Once this has been done, the tap is opened and the wine starts to flow under gravity into the barrel below. Pumps are not generally used in this operation.

Once the level of the wine reaches the level of the esquive, the flow is stopped. The bottom of the barrel contains the lees and so the barrel is tilted and the wine tipped into a metal funnel. Using a glass and the gentle light of a candle, the clarity of the wine is checked. As soon as the wine starts to appear cloudy, decanting is stopped. The second barrel is filled with clean wine and is returned to the ageing area where it ages for a further six months. The original barrel, emptied of the lees ("cloudiness"), is cleaned in accordance with the procedure described earlier and is returned to the racking area so that it can be filled again.

There are other ways of carrying out this process which are simpler and cheaper. One such method is racking by inserting a tube which draws out the wine using a small pump. Another option is not to decant but to top up the barrels every six months to avoid vinegarisation. This system necessitates extremely thorough filtering before the wine is bottled to clean out all the sediments from the ageing process.

The racking process. Once the bung is removed and a tap inserted, the wine flows under gravity into the barrel below. Meanwhile, the racker examines the wine in a glass by candlelight to see when "cloudiness" starts to appear. At that moment the decanting is stopped and only the clean wine continues the ageing process.

Although both systems are feasible in certain cases, neither is suitable for long ageing since they do not satisfy one or more of the three reasons for racking, namely to take the wine off the lees in a natural way, to monitor the quality of each barrel by hand and to oxygenate the wine to give it life until the next racking.

The number and frequency of rackings is determined by the oenologist and depends on various factors but, as a general rule, it is carried out every six months. As result of the volume of evaporate, this timetable has been found to be best for avoiding vinegarisation.

Proper control of the ageing process of wine necessitates monitoring on both an analytical and sensory level. During ageing, samples are taken from the barrels during each racking. It is essential to control free SO_2 levels and to carry out any adjustments necessary to keep the concentration within the range of 20-25 mg/l. Levels below this range may be too low to protect the wine from oxidation or from the growth of acetic or lactic bacteria or yeasts. On the other hand, higher levels may halt the wine's development. Likewise, regular tastings and analysis of volatile acidity make it possible to monitor whether the wine is developing correctly and, thus, to act if a problem is detected.

Systems do exist which can accelerate and cut the costs of a process as expensive as barrel ageing and which aim to give the wine similar, albeit not identical, characteristics to those which emerge during barrel ageing. Economic factors, oenological research and the New World styles have all encouraged the use of these techniques.

MICRO-OXYGENATION first appeared in France at the end of the 20th century as a result of the empirical studies carried out by Michel Moutounet which were then put into practice in the Madiran region by a group of vine growers who decided to experiment with the controlled introduction of oxygen in their wines produced from Tannat grapes. These grapes, which are very rich in tannins, produced a very strong sensation of dryness in the mouth after barrel ageing. The wine makers introduced small, controlled quantities of oxygen into their wines and then observed that the wines developed better and more slowly, retained their colour for longer, improved in structure and retained the fruity characteristics of the young wines. Based on these findings, the wine growing auxiliary industry threw itself into designing ways of methods of putting these results into practice on a large scale.

Micro-oxygenation is based on calculated oxygenation which slowly introduces oxygen at a slower rate than that at which the oxygen reacts with the wine, which stops it dissolving in the wine and facilitates the retention of various compounds, primarily the aromatic ones. There are various possible applications of this technology in oenology, such as introducing oxygen at the start of alcohol fermentation to promote yeast growth, introducing oxygen during ageing on the lees of white wines to provide greater structure and aromatic freshness, reducing wine times in barrel, speeding up the ageing process, etc.

COMPOUNDS DERIVED FROM OAK. Using fragments of oak to speed up and reduce the costs of ageing has been recognised since the time of Pasteur, when the master wine-makers were in the habit of using fragments of wood to give their wines the flavours and aromas of oak. Today there are various possibilities, such as oak granules (grains of oak wood in bags which have the effect of an infusion), shavings or chips (brittle-looking fragments of wood of some 10mm which may or may not have been toasted), oak fragments (bigger than shavings and lozenge shaped) or immersion of lozenges, thin strips or planks (which are larger and are submerged and anchored at the bottom of the vats or attached to the walls)

OUR CONCLUSION is that the studies carried out to date show that it has not been possible to achieve the same levels of quality using substitutes as with the slow and painstaking technique of barrel ageing, with the only positive outcomes being a reduction in the costs and a speeding up of the ageing process.

Wine is not aged in barrels so that it will taste of oak but because the quiet maturing allows for the development of aspects, qualities and sensations which only the slow and natural passage of time can bring.

Oak shavings (chips) of differing sizes to give the wine an artificial bouquet of ageing.

Collection of corks from the different bodegas in our Group, already stamped and prepared for the bottling process.

THE CORK

Fine example of a Portuguese cork oak, after removal of the sheets of cork. It will be at least another nine years now before the next removal of sheets can take place.

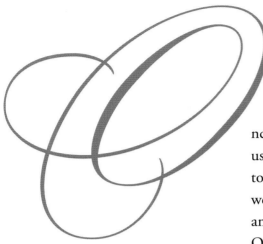

nce the wines have been bottled, it is necessary to seal the bottles using a system which will stop the wine escaping and enable it to be stored and to develop. Traditionally natural cork closures were used but towards the end of the 20th century new systems and materials came into fashion. La Rioja Alta, S.A., Torre de Oña, S.A. and Áster use only natural cork to stopper bottles as it allows the slow and satisfactory development of our wines. Lagar de Fornelos, S.A. which makes the Albariño wine Lagar de Cervera, is testing new seals such as *Stelvin caps (*screw tops), in certain markets.

HISTORY AND PRODUCTION OF CORK CLOSURES

Cork has a number of physical and chemical properties which make it suitable for use as a closure in the wine industry. It is impermeable, can be easily compressed so as to facilitate its being pushed into the neck of a bottle and, lastly, it is elastic, i.e. it recovers its original shape after being compressed which means that it stops liquid escaping from the container.

This ancient material was already used by the Romans and during the medieval period, although the first records of its use date from the 16th century, perhaps because of the experiences of the thousands of pilgrims who travelled across Northern Spain along the Camino de Santiago. According to legend, they included Dom Perignon who, after a journey to the Abbey of San Feliu de Guixols in Catalonia at the end of the 17th century, began to use cork stoppers to seal the bottles of wine produced at his abbey at Hautvilliers.

Thereafter, cork was for many years the only form of closure used. However, at the end of the last century, and due primarily to problems with bad odours and flavours which cork very occasionally imparted to a wine, other styles of closures started to be used, particularly ones made from a variety

Stripping off a sheet of cork.

of different materials. Thus silicon closures of different shapes and colours made their debut, followed by technical closures.

Cork is extracted from the bark of the cork oak (*Quercus suber*), which is grown in the Iberian Peninsula, principally in the Mediterranean costal region, in Portugal and in Extremadura and Andalucía. Like all the species of the genus *Quercus*, it is characteristically long lived (it can live more than 200 years) and has a productive life of more than 150 years. It is also grown to a lesser extent in Algeria, Morocco, France, Tunisia and Italy.

Cork is made up of layers of dead suberose tissue cells which are created as the tree grows outwards and form on top of one another year after year, creating a protective bark. Some 25 years after the cork oak is planted the "male" or virgin" cork is harvested for the first time. This is very poor quality cork in terms of producing stoppers because it has a large number of pores and is uneven. The second harvest, the "female" one, takes place 9 years later and produces material which is suitable for manufacturing stoppers. Subsequent harvests then take place at intervals of between 9 and 12 years.

The production process involves various stages:

HARVEST. This is carried out during the first days of summer, when the entire tree is full of sap moving through the conductive vessels. It is done by hand using an axe with a curved blade to slice off the sheets of cork.

SEASONING THE SHEETS. The sheets are stacked outside for between one and two years, during which time the cork is washed clean by rainwater.

BOILING. The sheets are gathered into bales which are boiled in special boiling tanks for 45 minutes which eliminates any possible parasites and mineral salts and tannins which might otherwise be transferred to the wine. Subsequently, the bales are stacked in hot, sealed drying areas for two to three weeks, in order to remove moisture.

CUTTING AND SELECTION OF THE CORK SHEETS. This involves removing the maderized part of the cork, the sheets which are damaged (cracks, yellow spots, green cork, etc.) and those which are not thick enough to be used for corks. Once the sheets have been graded, they are stored in the production area for a further two to three years, after which they are again boiled in order to introduce the moisture necessary to facilitate cutting by machine.

SLICING. This is the process in which the graded sheets are cut into strips which are a similar depth to the size of the final corks.

PUNCHING. The strips are punched out with a slightly larger diameter than that of the final cork.

SELECTING THE CORKS. The first criterion is that of quality and the corks are checked by automatic machines which grade their quality on the basis of imperfections and defects.

WASHING. The corks are washed, sterilised and given a uniform appearance. Nowadays systems such as autoclaves and extractors are used to reduce the cork chloroanisole content (which imparts a mildew smell to the wines).

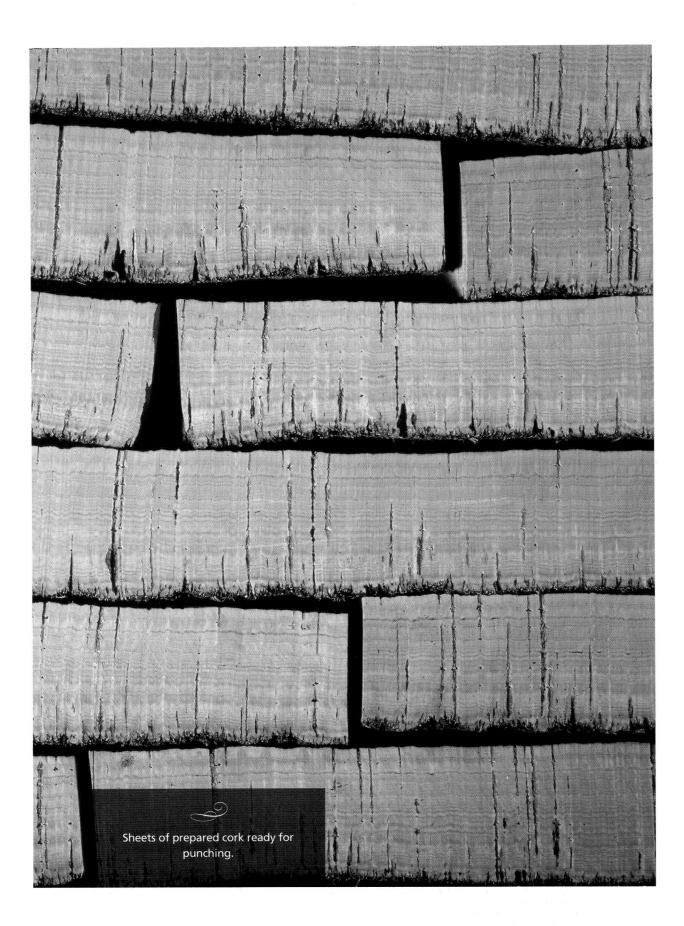

Sheets of prepared cork ready for punching.

CLASSIFICATION. The corks are graded again, with stricter criteria, either by hand or using a semi-automated process. They are graded by quality and although each producer will have its own standards, generally the following grading scale is used, in order of quality: Flor; Extra; Super-extra; Superior; First; Second; Third; Fourth, etc.

MARKING. The corks are marked with personalised stamps for each client which is done either by branding or with food-quality ink.

TREATMENT OF SURFACE AREA. This involves applying a paraffin compound which aids the cork's insertion into the bottle neck and its later removal and also increases air-tightness. Other products which may be applied include food-grade silicones or combinations of silicon and paraffin wax.

PACKING. Generally carried out using hermetically sealed polythene bags of 1,000 corks.

CORK RELATED DEFECTS

Defects arising out of corking can be classified into two major groups. The first relates to DEFECTS FROM THE MECHANICAL CORKING OPERATION. These include distortions of the cork (caused by malfunction of the corking machine, which may lead on occasion to a loss of wine and a poor external appearance), cork dust in the wine, bent corks, problems removing the cork (this may occur as a result of an abnormally narrow bottle neck or overly large cork, although the most common cause is poor distribution of the product used to treat the surface of the cork), sunken corks (caused by excessive pressure from the corking machine or excessive treatment of the surface), high corks (caused by insufficient pressure in the corking machine, an overly ligneous cork or one which is too large), corks which twist and fall apart when being removed (poor adhesion between cork and glass, with the same causes as for sunken corks), oozing (caused by a loss of cork volume and, in the majority of cases, leading to a fall in the quality of the wine because of excessive oxidation when the affected wine is exposed to the air).

A SINGLE PROBLEM WITH A CORK MAY RUIN YEARS OF WORK BY A WINE MAKER

The second group of defects, and the more serious, are those DEFECTS WHICH AFFECT THE QUALITY OF THE WINE. Chief amongst these defects is the bad taste which may be imparted to the wine, the problem of TCA cork taint, known as "corked" although in reality a good cork does not smell like this. It is the most well-known and the most serious although at present that are no lawful methods which would enable it to be eliminated. It is a defect which arises when the cork, or some other element, transmits a molecule known as TCA (2,4,6-trichloroanisole) to the wine with a perception threshold in wine between 5 and 10 nanograms/litre. The molecule makes its way into the cork in a variety of ways (through washing with chlorine, use of organochloride insecticides on the cork oaks, etc.). There are other molecules in cork

The sheet is punched to produce corks with a slightly larger diameter than their final one. ◯ Having been selected, washed and graded, the corks are branded with the logos and wording of each bodega.

which may impart a smell or taste similar to that of TCA but which have a higher perception threshold and appear sporadically. This second group of defects also includes oxidation and reduction defects, which are explained in Chapter 13 which covers ageing in bottle.

ALTERNATIVES TO CORK

Cork has enjoyed pre-eminence as a closure in bottles of wine by virtue of it being the only available material which combines the qualities necessary to ensure that the bottles are properly sealed. It is due precisely to its ability to ensure air-tightness that oxygen is unable to get into the bottle, which slows down the natural process of oxidation of the wine and thus allows it to develop properly. Nevertheless, cork does have certain disadvantages which may not be obvious: the bark of the cork oak is a natural material and corks do therefore vary. It is also a scarce material which is difficult to produce and is expensive.

As a consequence, new and alternative closure systems are now available on the market, of which the most notable are metal screw caps, synthetic closures and technical and semi-synthetic closures. These all have a common aim which is to reproduce the advantages of cork without suffering any of it's disadvantages.

Indeed synthetic closures have become very popular, particularly in the Anglo-Saxon market, as have technical and semi-synthetic closures. These may be made of cork (the One-Plus-One) or have an agglomerated body and natural cork discs at either end the Twin Top) or be made of a mixture of compressed cork dust (the Altec®). The most recent is the Diam® which is a unique mixture of cork granules and microspheres which give these technical corks excellent mechanical characteristics. The screw cap is a very popular choice in the New World, particularly for red wines of short ageing. In the United Kingdom it is a commonly found closure on white wines, including on our very own Lagar de Cervera.

The tables on the following page set out some of the advantages and disadvantages of one or other type of closure.

OTHER TYPES OF CLOSURE CANNOT ALWAYS GUARANTEE OPTIMUM DEVELOPMENT OF AGED WINES.

THE CORK ,WHOSE HISTORY STRETCHES BACK MORE THAN 500 YEARS, IS STILL THE BEST OPTION.

CORK CLOSURE		TECHNICAL OR SEMI-SYNTHETIC CLOSURES	
Advantages	Disadvantages	Advantages	Disadvantages
Traditional Excellent image Proven efficacy Easy to remove Simple automation use Enables positive development of the wine	TCA possible Inconsistent material, with considerable variety between corks Oxidation possible Requires a corkscrew Bottles must be stored flat	Looks like cork Consistency Easy to remove Easily adapted to different corking machines	TCA possible Oxidation possible Requires a corkscrew Bottles must be stored flat

SYNTHETIC CLOSURES		METAL CAPSULE OR SCREW CAP	
Advantages	Disadvantages	Advantages	Disadvantages
Consistency Free of TCA Easily adapted to different corking machines Bottles can be stored upright	Possible image problem Oxidation possible Possible smell of plastic Requires a corkscrew Problems with removal have been reported	Consistency Proven efficacy with white wines Maintains freshness Easy to remove No need for a corkscrew Bottles can be stored upright	Possible image problem Untested over long periods of ageing of red wine Reduction problems possible Requires suitable bottles and equipment

It is our long-held view that the choice of a good cork is a vitally important factor for our wines. The huge human and financial commitment from the vineyard to the moment that the consumer opens the bottle should not be ruined by problems with the cork.

La Rioja Alta, S.A., only buys corks from well-established suppliers who have passed the validation process. Only the highest quality is acceptable for all of our wines and economic considerations are irrelevant.

The purchasing process begins with a study of the current year's requirements. Suppliers are furnished with a copy of the strict technical specifications which the corks must meet, with these specifications being revised every year. Once an order has been placed, a visit is made to the supplier's premises to choose the batches required, from which random samples are collected and sent both to an independant laboratory in Bordeaux, which will issue either a certificate of approval or of rejection of the sample, and to our own laboratory. If the sample is approved by both laboratories, the order is given to brand the corks.

When the corks are delivered, further random sampling is carried out so that another quality control test can be done. These monitoring processes are carried out both in our internal laboratory and in various other laboratories. Once all the tests have been completed successfully, the batch is accepted and is sent to be used in the bottling process.

Furthermore, throughout the bottling process, ageing in bottle, labelling and the period that the bottles of wine are stored in our facilities, the wine is checked from an organoleptic and physico-chemical point of view to ensure its quality.

Despite all the attention and complex processes, obviously checking every cork would involve destroying it and it is, therefore, simply not feasible to do. The monitoring process is, therefore, a statistical one. This means that a bad cork may "sneak" into a good batch and a problem with that bottle will eventually materialise. Monitoring efforts are restricted to minimising this type of incident since it is accepted that it is not possible at the present time to eliminate them completely.

Ageing in bottle requires time, stillness and mystery and it is the foundation on which the aromas, the roundness and the smoothness of a fine wine are built.

AGEING
IN BOTTLE

Shaft and Craft
(Great Britain, ca.1670).

Onion bottle
(Great Britain, ca.1685).

Onion bottle
(Low Countries, 1720-1750).

Flowerpot type
(Great Britain, 1750-1760).

Flattened cylinder
(Great Britain, ca. 1777).

Triple mould
(Great Britain, 1830-1850).

Cylindrical bottle
(France, ca. 1840).

Cylindrical bottle
(France, end of 19th C).

Cylindrical bottle
(France, 1903).

consumer often asks himself whether keeping wine in the bottle serves any purpose. This chapter will endeavour to explain the important changes which take place in a wine in its colour, aroma and flavour during the period it is resting in a glass bottle and why, exactly, glass has reigned supreme.

BOTTLE PRODUCTION

A BRIEF HISTORY OF THE BOTTLE

Amphorae, skins, eartherware jugs, wineskins, barrels… have all been used over the course of the centuries to transport and market wine. There have been many and varied methods, some more common than others, but all with a common enemy: oxygen. The danger of vinegarisation or of the wine turning rancid has shaped the wine industry since the days when the most prized wines of Antiquity came from the Mediterranean area and routinely had an alcohol content above 13° which meant that they could be transported slowly without too much risk to such a precious cargo.

Fortunately, the glass bottle was born. With its sealing qualities allied to the more recent introduction of sulphur to eliminate the oxygen contained within the barrels, it works its own miracle. A quality wine, which may only have had a moderate alcohol content, could now be easily transported to areas further afield than the Mediterranean area of old.

The term "bottle" comes from the Latin "butticula", the diminutive of the term "buttis" which meant barrel. Clearly since its very creation and its early artisan production there have been many changes in its shape, all moving towards a longer and narrower neck. One shape became the norm and standard at the turn of the 20th century, thanks to the introduction of mechanical processes in manufacturing and bottling systems. Nowadays, it is used quasi-universally on account of its many properties which have made it unique in the preservation of wine. Many substitutes have been contemplated, to avoid the problems of its seeming fragility but this is without doubt a lesser evil when compared with for example its precious impermeability to the dreaded oxygen and its acknowledged resistance against other elements such as light, water or chemical components.

Until the 17th century, the main concern of English wine merchants was to sell wine as quickly as possible, because the barrels in which wine was stored and transported failed to keep it in good condition, resulting in the wine turning to vinegar in a very short space of time. Over the course of the century, a revolution took place firstly with the bottle and then with the arrival of a secure method of sealing it – the cork. Until that point, bottles were either of ceramic or clear glass for serving the wine at table, but these were fragile and expensive. A cheaper way of manufacturing bottles was to throw handfuls of common salt into the oven during firing. This then reacted with the clay minerals and produced a vitreous finish which was a grayish or brownish colour. As long as glass remained delicate, it would remain a luxury and bottles continued to be made in the same way as drinking glasses and glass used for windows.

USING GLASS AS A CONTAINER FOR WINE CAUSED A REVOLUTION IN ALL AREAS OF THE WINE BUSINESS

The demand for glass grew throughout the 17th century, so much so that the English monarch prohibited glass makers from burning wood in their ovens, mainly because this practice had led to widespread deforestation. King James I of England proclaimed a degree which compelled any manufacturer using such an oven to change the fuel. In 1620 Sir Robert Mansell founded his main premises close to the most famous mines, those of Newcastle upon Tyne, and started an explosion in the number of ovens used to manufacture glass for jugs and windows. Coal produced higher temperatures in the ovens, leading to the discovery that the higher the temperature, the stronger the glass produced.

In 1630 Kenelm Digby, a writer, alchemist and privateer, began to manufacture thicker bottles which were heavier, stronger, darker and, most importantly, cheaper close to the mines of Newnham on Severn. These bottles were globular with a high, tapered neck and a collar, to which the stopper was tied. Digby managed to increase the temperature of the coal-fired ovens still further, using a wind tunnel which meant that glass containing a higher ratio of sand to potash and lime could be manufactured. This new mixture produced a glass which was darker, either a brownish colour or dark olive green, perhaps even almost black, because of the coal fumes, which increased the strength of the glass and endowed it with an ability to protect against light, although this latter characteristic was not appreciated until much later. Although Digby was imprisoned some years later for being a monarchist and a Catholic which led to other speculators taking the credit for his invention, in 1662 Parliament decided to recognise Digby as the inventor of the glass bottle.

Following this discovery, the problem remained of finding a material to seal the bottle, stop leakage of liquid and so increase storage potential. Initially, closures were made of glass to fit the neck of the bottle, then ground and covered in oil. It was not until much later, in the 17th century that cork started to be used.

Finally, all that remained was to invent a way of removing the cork cleanly. The first mention of a corkscrew dates from 1681 by Nehemiah Grew, a doctor and botanist, who described it as "a metal worm used to pull corks out of bottles". Until then, the "metal worms" had been used to remove bullets which had got stuck in firearms.

MANUFACTURE

Glass is produced by solidifying a mixture of silica, sand and recycled glass which has been subjected to temperatures of more than 1,000°C. The table on the right shows the main constituents used in the manufacture of glass bottles. Other constituents include recovered glass, also known as "calcin" or "groisil" and certain additives which are used to colour the glass, such as iron oxide, nickel, iron, molybdenum, chromium, manganese, silver, etc.

CONSTITUENT	QUANTITY (%)
White silica	46%
Sand	15%
Sodium carbonate	15%
Limestone	11%
Sodium sulphate	9%
Pyrite	2%
Carbon dust	1%
Ferromanganese	1%

The most common bottle colours today are:

DARK TOPAZ BLACK, used for fortified wines; also used for our Áster wine.
AMBER, used in the beer industry and for certain wines.
DEAD LEAF GREEN, used for example for Lagar de Cervera.
DARK GREEN anti-UV (ultra-violet rays), used a great deal for red wines, including those of La Rioja Alta, S.A. and Torre de Oña.
SEMICLEAR, used for brandies and liqueurs, white and rosé wines.
CLEAR, colourless, used for white and rosé wines.

The colour of the glass is very important for the wine, since light, or more precisely ultra-violet rays, adversely affects a wine's quality (light sickness, premature ageing). For this reason, wine is put into bottles in colours which filter out these rays. The best colour for filtering out rays is amber, then dark green anti-UV and lastly colourless or clear glass.

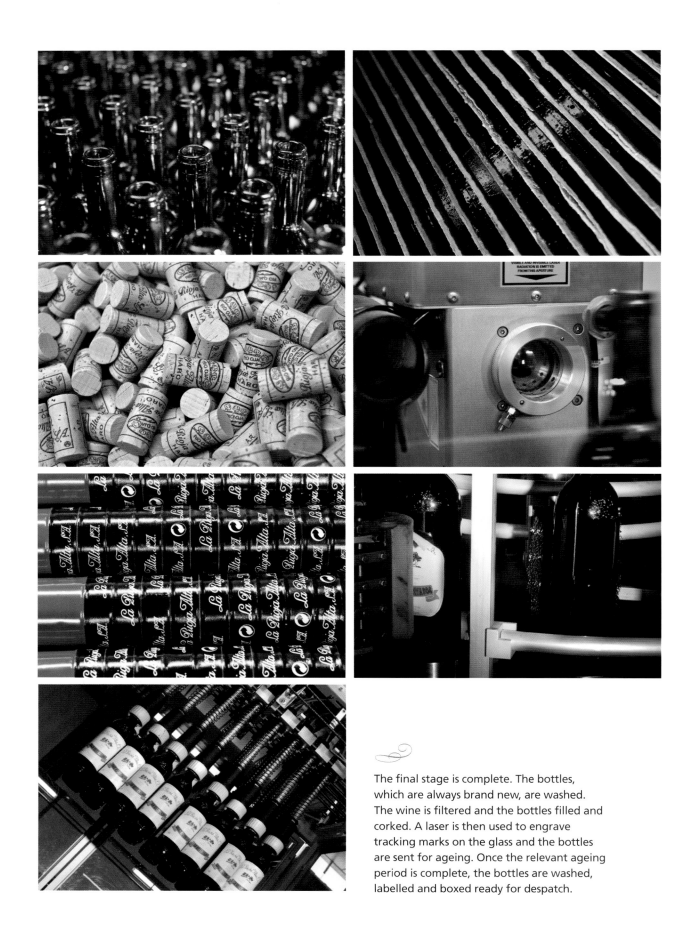

The final stage is complete. The bottles, which are always brand new, are washed. The wine is filtered and the bottles filled and corked. A laser is then used to engrave tracking marks on the glass and the bottles are sent for ageing. Once the relevant ageing period is complete, the bottles are washed, labelled and boxed ready for despatch.

TYPES OF BOTTLE

Traditionally, the most commonly used bottles are:

BORDEAUX. A cylindrical bottle with high shoulders and a long neck. Used for Viña Alberdi, Viña Arana, Gran Reserva 904, Gran Reserva 890, Marqués de Haro, Barón de Oña, Áster, Lagar de Cervera and Club de Cosecheros.

BURGUNDY. A cylindrical body, wider than a Bordeaux bottle, with sloped shoulders. Used for Viña Ardanza.

CHAMPAGNE BOTTLE. Very similar to a Burgundy bottle, made of green glass which is thicker in order to contain the high pressure of the sparkling wine.

FLUTE OR RHINE BOTTLE. Similar to a Burgundy bottle but longer and more slender. Very commonly used for German wines.

SHERRY BOTTLE. Very similar to a Bordeaux bottle, but with straighter and higher shoulders.

PORT BOTTLE. Similar to a Sherry bottle, with straight and flat shoulders and a bulb in the neck.

FRANCONIA BOTTLE. Flattened, short and with a round base and neck. Very typical of white Franken wines.

BOTTLING

It is first necessary to prepare the wine for bottling so as to bring together the necessary conditions to ensure the wine's microbiological and physico-chemical stability, without adversely affecting its present and future organoleptic qualities. To do this requires both an extensive knowledge of its history and a forecast of its development.

The wine is first examined by tasting and its main components are analysed: the alcohol content, total acidity, pH, organic acids, residual sugars, sulphur dioxide levels etc. A series of laboratory tests is also carried out to establish its microbiological and physico-chemical stability so as to avoid the risk of future precipitation.

Then, any treatments which may be necessary to maintain the wine's stability without adversely affecting its quality are administered, including the following three:

CLARIFYING OR FINING PROCESS. Various substances are added which make the wine very cloudy and lead to the formation of large particles which draw all the particles in suspension down to the bottom, leaving the wine clean and bright. This procedure eliminates the possibility of the particles in suspension precipitating in the future and causing undesirable lees. A number of products are used, such as gelatines, egg albumin, caseins, bentonites and oenological tannins. Moreover, the clarification process improves the organoleptic properties of wines.

FILTRATION. This involves the physical separation of the particles in suspension in the wine using filters. The filters are membranes made of a combination of materials with different sized pores. The filtration process enables inorganic particles (salts, particularly colloidal particles) and live or dead micro-organisms (yeasts, bacteria and fungi) to be removed.

ADDITION OF COADJUVANTS OR ADDITIVES. Generally preservatives are used which prevent oxidation of the wine and the growth of undesirable microorganisms. Sulphur dioxide (SO_2) and ascorbic acid are the most commonly used.

Once these processes have been carried out, the wine is sent for bottling, with all the necessary materials having already been assembled: bottles, corks and storage cases.

The new bottles are delivered to the bodega and then put through the bottle washer which washes the inside using a high-pressure water jet. Once drained, they are sent to the filling plant. Filling is done using gravity and foaming or spillage of wine is avoided by controlling the filling rate. Once the bottles are full, they move on to the corking machine which inserts the corks, creating a pre-determined vacuum which will avoid excess pressure in the bottles, which can cause leakages or the cork to pop out if the pressure within the bottle is too high. Lastly, the bottles are put into metal cases which, once filled and closed, are rotated so that the bottles are kept in a horizontal position until they are labelled.

DEVELOPMENT OF THE WINE IN THE BOTTLE

Ageing in bottle represents a improving development which adds complexity and refinement in an environment free of oxygen (reduction). The time required to achieve this improvement in quality varies greatly depending on the type of wine and may be a few years or several decades. The "great wines" are characterised by a long ageing whilst more modest wines require very little ageing time to develop all of their qualities. Ageing potential is very closely connected with the chemical composition of the wine and, more precisely, with its phenolic composition.

It is thought that ageing in bottle goes through three stages: a maturing phase, a peak phase and a phase of decline.

DURING THE MATURING PHASE, a wine's sensorial quality slowly increases. The quality may sometimes fluctuate if the wine goes through "reduction" or "bottle sickness", which is the result of a lack of oxygen and may lead to the development of certain unpleasant smelling molecules (thiols). During this first phase, the wine loses fruitiness and may appear hard and astringent. Ordinarily this phase lasts a few months, after which the wine slowly recovers. Varieties such as Tempranillo, Cariñena or Syrah are more vulnerable to this problem. Furthermore, certain aspects of the production process, such as long maceration phases, inadequate ageing or wines being stored on the lees, can increase the likelihood of reduction.

DURING THE PEAK PHASE, the wine reaches its optimum level, developing a wide range of aromas and flavours which form the bouquet. The length of this phase depends on the intrinsic characteristics of the wine, the way in which it has been produced, the barrel ageing and what is known in the wine industry as the "harvest effect", that is to say the vine growing and climatic conditions in which the vegetative cycle of the vine actually took place that year.

DURING THE DECLINE PHASE the wine slowly loses the characteristics which define its quality. It becomes drier and loses body and structure. This organoleptic change is accompanied by precipitation in the bottles. At the same time, the colour changes to brick red or orangey yellow, with the purplish hues in red wines disappearing completely and the colour of white wines darkening to intense gold shades. These progressive changes in colour are influenced by the phenol composition of the wine. In general, the colour can be seen as a marker of ageing, with very old wines being an intense yellow/brick red colour. Wine develops slowly at 12°C, more rapidly at 18°C and may develop too quickly at higher temperatures. Equally, intensive oxidation caused by a porous cork which is not airtight can lead to the total and rapid degradation of the wine. This is the reason why, during ageing in bottle, the temperature variations between summer and winter must be minimised so as to avoid changes in liquid volumes which contribute to the drawing in of air which adversely affects the development of the wine.

ONE RULE GOVERNS THE DEVELOPMENT OF WINE IN BOTTLE: THE BEST WINE IS NOT ALWAYS PRODUCED WHEN WE MOST EXPECT IT

CHEMICAL ANALYSIS

During ageing in bottle, various chemical reactions take place.

There are polymerisation reactions between tannins and condensation reactions between anthocyanins and tannins. These reactions continue for the entire duration of the ageing in bottle and, at the end of this phase, cause the precipitation of polymers which will give the wine ductility.

In terms of the colour, the shade intensifies. The free anthocyanins disappear and while there is little change to the intensity of the colour, the hue develops orangey red or brick red tones. During barrel ageing the anthocyanins combine with the tannins and form red/purple complexes. During ageing in bottle one part of these complexes develops into orangey structures while another part may precipitate, causing lees which adhere to the inside of the bottle. The speed of these reactions varies greatly and depends on the ratio of existing tannins and anthocyanins. Thus, the colour of a wine rich in anthocyanins which combined with tannins during barrel ageing will develop more slowly in the bottle

All our brands and sizes….. a very fine family in which the different personalities complement one another and all have something to contribute.

than that of another wine with a lower level of combined anthocyanins. The ageing of a wine in bottle is a process of progressive cleansing that depends on the polyphenol levels in the wine. Great wines which age well are rich in phenol compounds, although this does not necessarily mean that all wines which are rich in polyphenols will be great wines. A wine which is hard and astringent at the bottling stage will still be hard and astringent even after several years.

Polysaccharides affect the stability of the polymers (the protective colloids) which are formed by reacting with the tannins in the wine to form tannin-polysaccharides. These help to soften the wine as long as their levels are not such as to transform them into a colloidal state which would then cause the them to precipitate. Great wines always contain a considerable quantity of polysaccharides, compared to more modest wines from the same harvest.

THE BOTTLE IS THE KEY TO THE DEVELOPMENT OF AROMAS AND THE WINE'S ROUNDNESS AND SMOOTHNESS

The behaviour of wines during ageing depends, therefore, on a series of factors relating to their composition. These factors are not limited to the polyphenol levels but also include the nature and the structure of the tannins as well as the tannin/anthocyanin reactions and the polysaccharide levels. Furthermore, the initial composition of the wine is altered by the ageing process, with new and complex structures forming that may slow down the wine cleansing process.

DEVELOPMENT OF AROMA OR BOUQUET

It has been noted that the bouquet of both red and white wines appears some time after bottling, generally after all the dissolved oxygen in the wine has reacted and reached a low level or, which amounts to the same thing, there is a low oxide reduction potential. This oxide reduction potential depends on the nature of the wine and the amount of sulphur added during bottling. The new bouquet arises out of complex reactions between the varietal aromas of the grape (primary aromas), those produced during alcohol and malolactic fermentation (secondary aromas) and, lastly, those connected with ageing (tertiary aromas).

These reactions multiply in inverse proportion to the fall in the oxide reduction potential of the wine and continue while its level is low. Warmer temperatures and light encourage conditions for reduction and hasten the process and can even modify it, although accelerated ageing rarely leads to balanced products. Slow development, which is the ideal reaction, requires temperatures below 20°C and shelter from the effects of light.

REDUCTION AND OXIDATION

In the case of ageing in bottle, the corking machine is responsible for ensuring the air-tightness of the system and will determine the reduction status of the wine. Where wine is stored in a container made of a porous material which is insufficiently airtight (such as PVC or polyethylene), the SO_2 leaks out and the wine dissolves a large quantity of oxygen, thereby hampering smooth development of the aroma. A glass bottle combined with a cork stopper provide a greater degree of air-tightness and there are notable differences in the quality of the aroma, because of the tiny amount of movement of oxygen in the wine.

While the development of the aroma of the majority of great wines is a function of the reduction phenomenon, the opposite phenomenon, known as "airing", is oxidative and is generally considered to happen accidentally, although in some case it can be deliberate as is the case with the oloroso and amontillado wines of Jerez. These two contrasting changes are reversible and disappear when faced with conditions which are the opposite of the conditions which created them. Airing eliminates the aroma and causes the wine to develop characteristics such as dark chocolate, bitterness, acridness and burning, as well as an organoleptic hardness. Aeration causes this phenomenon which may even result in "woodiness" with white wines and "rancidity" with red wines if there is considerable oxidation. Airing, which benefits from warmer temperatures, can be achieved more easily during the wine operations of the summer than those of the winter. Aldehydes are always formed during those operations where the wine is in contact with the air, particularly acetaldehyde which is responsible for the "aired" characteristic which then disappears rapidly when SO_2 is added.

MANAGEMENT OF THE WINE IN BOTTLE: TEMPERATURE AND HUMIDITY

The locations where the bottles are to be stored must provide temperature and humidity conditions which enable the wine to develop correctly. The bottles are placed in the metal containers which are then turned so that the bottles are horizontal. This enables the corks to remain moist and so prevents them drying out and losing their air-tightness. The temperature of the bottle racks must be kept relatively low, between 9°C and 12°C throughout the year. It is important to avoid sharp temperature variations between winter and summer, as these can hasten the development of the wine.

It is also important to maintain relative humidity levels between 70% and 80%, since below this levels leakage from the bottles may occur as the corks dry out. Alternatively, if relative humidity is high then fungi may grow on the surface of the corks. These fungi do not affect the quality of the wine but they are not aesthetically pleasing. In order to achieve the necessary humidity and temperature levels, underground premises are used which naturally provide such conditions. Historically, during the hot summer months, the floors of the storage premises were watered so as to maintain humidity levels. Nowadays, humidification and air conditioning systems are commonly installed in bodegas.

Different bottle sizes: Split (0.187 l); half bottle (0.375 l); standard (0.75 l); magnum (1.5 l); double magnum (3 l); Jeroboam (4.5 l); Rehoboam (5.5 l); box (5 l); Imperial (6 l); Salmanazar (9 l); Balthazar (12 l); Nebuchadnezzar (15 l). For champagne, which uses a different nomenclature, there are also the Melchior or Solomon (18 l), Sovereign (15 l), Primat (27 l) or Melchizedek (30 l).

Other factors which have to be managed include the hygiene of the ambient air in the bottle storage areas, which must be free of bad smells. Automatic air extraction systems which renew the air are used to achieve this, or alternatively natural air inlets which allow air currents to refresh the air in the premises. These air currents also control humidity and temperature in a non-mechanised manner. It is common practice in bodegas to keep the doors and windows of the bottle storage areas open during the cool summer nights. This not only allows the temperature to be controlled but also refreshes the ambient air.

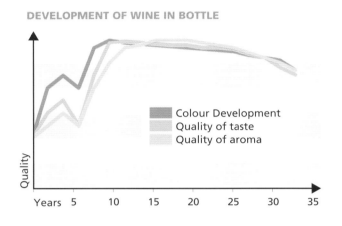

DEVELOPMENT OF WINE IN BOTTLE

Colour Development
Quality of taste
Quality of aroma

Quality

Years 5   10   15   20   25   30   35

The lighting must be the minimum which is absolutely necessary to stack and unstack the boxes. Lamps must be fluorescent, plastic-covered and give off very little heat. It is also necessary to carry out pest control measures in the bottle storage areas using special lamps and traps. Moths, or more precisely moth larvae, may attack the corks and make holes which can then lead to leakage of wine. Lastly, it is essential to keep the bottles orderly and perfectly clean, removing any broken bottles or any other material which may cause bad smells.

WINE IN THE HOME

As in the bodega, the ideal conditions for storing wine are those which take into account the humidity, temperature, light conditions, absence of smells and parasites and the position of the wine. Thus, the cellar or basement in the home should mimic as far as possible the conditions in a bodega.

Firstly, if at all possible, a north facing underground, or partially underground, area is preferable. The partitions or walls should be such as to ensure that the room is insulated and sound-proofed, should be white and, if possible, made of a Tyrolean cement/gravel mix. Insulation systems using fibreglass or expanded polyurethane achieve such objectives very well. The floor plays a very important hygrometric role and a material which can absorb humidity is, therefore, recommended, such as porous ceramic floor tiles, although a better solution is compacted earth spread with river sand.

Adequate ventilation must also be available, to enable air renewal and maintain suitable humidity levels in the cellar. Storing bottles in the kitchen or larder is not recommended, since the smoke, high temperatures and smells may cause a significant loss of quality. The dining room or sitting room are also unsuitable storage areas, with the noise and temperature adversely affecting the wine.

With some reservations, the most suitable areas would be an internal room or the hallway, where it would be possible to build a small, suitably insulated bottle rack. Another alternative would be to install a storage cabinet.

To store wines, certain basic rules must be complied with:

- The ideal storage temperature is between 10°C and 15°C, with the minimum temperature being 7°C and the maximum 18°C.
- The wine must be protected from temperature fluctuations, so the maximum daily variation should be no greater than 2°C and the relative humidity should be between 70% and 80%.
- Bottles should be stored in a horizontal position, in bottle racks made of wood or other material which does not conduct heat.
- Light should be avoided as much as possible and it is, therefore, important to use portable lamps with carbon filaments or cold indirect light.
- Wines cannot withstand foreign smells, such as paint, cooking smells, cold meats, fruit etc. and noise and vibration are its sworn enemies.
- Aeration and ventilation of the wine storage facility are both important and necessary.
- Lastly, it is very helpful to keep a "cellar book" or log, to note the name of the wine, the type, harvest, date of purchase, price and any other information which might be considered useful.

Domestic cellar, with different sections for boxes, cases, glasses, special bottles, books on wine.....

Once a wine has finished the ageing in bottle phase, it is time for it to be presented in an elegant and polished manner. During the ageing process, bottles get dirty and dusty and it is necessary to clean them by putting them through an "external washer". After this, the bottle is dressed.

The capsule has various roles: it serves to guarantee the wine in the bottle, it keeps the external surface of the cork and the neck of the bottle clean and in good condition and, lastly, it adds value to the design and presentation. It is not clear whether wine in a bottle with a capsule improves to a greater or lesser extent than wine in a bottle without a capsule and we are carrying out research into this.

Historically, this extra protection was provided by placing sealing wax over the mouths of those bottles intended for ageing, be it a longer or a short ageing, so as to avoid wine leaking from the cork and to reduce oxygenation. There were, however, problems with applying the wax and then opening the seal, so we started to use capsules made of lead. For environmental reasons, lead was later substituted for tin, which is the material now used for all the capsules on bottles from La Rioja Alta, S.A. The capsules are made from a single piece of pure tin and are adorned with various motifs and colours. The capping machine is in the labelling line, between the external washer and the labelling machine. These machines include a system for storing the capsules, mechanisms for placing them on the bottles and a device for straightening and adjusting them to the neck of the bottles.

The bottles are then dressed with the labelling elements. The term "labelling" covers the name, logos, pictures, brands or any other description which characterises a product and features on the bottle, and it comprises:

LABELS. They carry all the compulsory information required under Community and national regulations, including the rules governing designation, appellation, presentation and protection of still wines, as well as other voluntary information. The most significant compulsory information includes the name of the product, nominal volume, details of the bottler or supplier, the Register of Bottlers number, the name of the Denominación de Origen, the batch number, the municipality and the country.

BACK LABELS. These include information which may be of interest to consumers of our wines or indeed details which are required by one of our clients, as is the case with back labels (or in fact labels) which have been personalised for a particular restaurant or business.

SEAL OR COLLAR OF THE REGULATORY BODY. This certifies that the wine is entitled to the designation "Denominación de Origen Calificada" from Rioja, Ribera del Duero, Rías Baixas or other, as appropriate.

PACKAGING. This term is taken to mean any type of wrapping on the bottles which serves to protect or decorate either the label or the wine. It can be made of paper, wire netting, cardboard, metal or can be a bag, case, box, etc. used to transport the bottles and then present them to the eventual consumer. In general the bottles are despatched in cardboard boxes holding either 6 or 12 bottles to distributors and restaurants or provided in cases containing 3 bottles to visitors to the bodega. A luxury presentation usually comprises a printed wooden box, which may or may not have been varnished, made in various sizes to hold different numbers of bottles. There is little diversity between bodegas throughout the world, although some present their bottles in metal boxes while others use more personalised and unusual containers. The Champagne region is probably the most sophisticated in this regard, with presentation styles which are really innovative and elegant.

Numbering
(if applicable)

Production run
(if applicable)

D.O. region

Brand name

Volume

Batch number

Bottler
registration
number

Seal of the
Regulatory
Body

Company
name

Municipality
and country

Alcohol
content

Painting by Marc Jesús which hangs in one of our dining rooms and was commissioned by the bodega. It represents the happiness, the sensuality and the enjoyment which should go hand in hand with tasting a good wine.

TASTING

Our Salon D. Guillermo incorporates facilities for both technical and practical tasting courses. It is also available for business functions, product presentations, meetings of boards of directors, etc.

asting is the part of oenology which every consumer lives intensely. All the senses are involved, wrapped up in memories, and it can be both a joyful and a complex experience. As with anything to do with the world of wine, it is as much an art as a science. At times it can even scare us. There is one basic principle to bear in mind: for a wine lover, the only important question is whether they like the wine or not.

HISTORY

Wine tasting is not a modern invention, having its roots far back in time. In 1312 Philippe the Beautiful created a wine association in Paris, called the "Courtier-Gourmet-Piqueurs de Vins", which still exists today. In 1793 the role of taster was defined for the first time in France as "the art of sampling wines". Nevertheless, the word "taste" can mean many things: to savour, to sample, to try, to test, to analyse, to appreciate, to relish, etc. It was Jean Ribereau-Gayon, the father of Modern Oenology, who defined the significance of wine tasting as "… to taste a wine with care in order to appreciate its quality; to submit it to examination by our senses, in particular those of taste and smell; to try and understand it by discovering its various qualities and defects. It is to study it, analyse it, describe it, judge it, classify it."

In Spain, the growth of taster associations began with the creation of the Denominaciones de Origen, which meant that the classification of wine had to go hand in hand with a sensory assessment carried out by a "group of specialised tasters". In the final third of the 20th century and at the same time as a huge expansion of the wine-producing industry, there was a surge in the publication of wine guides and specialised publications, which had and continues to have important repercussions for tasting. At the same time there was a rise in the number of "media gurus" who, through their writings, turned themselves into opinion formers and creators of consumer trends.

Tasting Room at Torre de Oña, S.A.

The various sensory stimuli of drink or food are the physical and/or chemical properties of which it is composed which, when perceived by the sense organs, become organoleptic qualities. Measuring these organoleptic properties is the first phase of tasting, the analysis and observation phase, with the second phase being the judging of quality.

Several senses are involved in the tasting process. The sensations arise out of diverse stimuli: visual, olfactory, taste, tactile, chemical and temperature. These sensations combine together and become confused when wine is drunk without paying attention to what is being drunk. For that reason, the aim of tasting is to separate, organise and identify some of the impressions that a wine produces. The following table sets out the senses involved.

ORGAN	SENSES AND SENSATIONS	CHARACTERISTICS PERCEIVED
Eye	Vision	Colour, limpidity
	Visual sensations	Fluidity, effervescence
Nose	Olfactory (orthonasal)	Aroma, bouquet
	Olfactory sensations	
	Olfactory (retronasal)	Aroma in the mouth
	Olfactory sensations	
Mouth	Taste	Taste
	Taste sensations	Astringency, causticity
	Mucosal reactions	Bubbliness
	Chemical sensitivity	
	Tactile sensations	Consistency, liquidity, fluidity, smoothness
	Heat sensations	Temperature

Tasting comprises four phases: (1) Observation through the senses; (2) description of perceptions; (3) composition in comparison with recognised standards; (4) lastly, reasoned judgment.

SIGHT

The colour of a wine depends on its ability to absorb in different ways the coloured rays which pass through it. A red wine is red-coloured because it captures green rays, whereas another wine is white because it absorbs violet light. The appearance of a wine provides information not only about its colour but also about its limpidity, fluidity, movement and CO_2 emissions. Thus, the mousse in a Cava or a Champagne and the way in which it fades and dissolves and the liveliness and effervescence of the bubbles are all important aspects when analysing it. The mousse should not be either dense nor creamy

The colour of wine changes substantially as the wine ages. The following photographs show several representative examples.

Young wine: ruby red, with a deep red rim on the meniscus.

Crianza: cherry red with a thin iodine layer at the edge.

Young white: straw-coloured yellow with a greenish tone. Colourless meniscus.

Reserva: cherry red with more intense iodine layer.

Gran Reserva: brick red with wide orangey-yellow layer and mahogany edges.

Blanco Reserva: golden yellow. Intense heart and little transparency.

233

but rather fine and dry, fading away within a few seconds without disappearing completely from the surface. The bubbles forming at the bottom of the glass should be small and form a small bead.

When one observes a glass of wine, having first carried out the typical circular movement to oxygenate it, a fine, transparent layer slides down the sides until it reaches the bottom. This is known as "the legs of the wine" and is more plentiful where the wine has a higher level of alcohol and glycerine and greater structure.

WINE	COLOUR
White	Greenish yellow
	Straw yellow
	Amber
	Golden yellow
Rosé	Pink
	Orangey pink
	Amber pink
	Onion skin
Red	Violet red
	Ruby red
	Deep red
	Brownish red

The colour is so determinative in the appearance of the wine that it can, on its own, define the wine type. It is for this reason that wines are referred to as whites (yellow or golden), reds (purple or ruby red), rosés and claretes.

The intensity of the colour is presumed to indicate the structure. A strong and dark colour is associated with wines with body and with a strong tannin expression. If the colour is weak (often referred to as "open colour"), the wine generally has a light appearance. This identification scheme is not necessarily correct. In fact, many wines such as those from Burgundy may have a light colour but excellent body and length.

The shade of a colour indicates a wine's degree of development and its age. A young red wine is a purple or ruby colour but once it has aged the shade darkens and it turns dark or brick red. A young white wine has pale yellow or green highlights which mature into golden amber tones.

Liveliness is another quality of a wine which depends to a greater or lesser extent on "the life left in a wine". A wine may be brilliant, honest, subdued or dead.

Rosé and clarete wines are intermediate to whites and reds and are not a mixture of the two (see Chapter 9). Their colours cover a broad spectrum of shades and hues, from yellows, reddish shades and pale reds. The colour known as "champagne" is typical of "blancs de noirs" wines (white wines made from black grapes) when they are very young.

THE NOSE

The nose recognises and classifies the volatile components of a wine. The volatile sensations evolve as air is inhaled. During an olfactory cycle of four to five seconds, there is a progressive increase in the sensations which reaches a peak, drops off and then slowly fades away.

The terms "aroma" and "bouquet" refer to pleasant smells, of varying intensity and complexity, which are given off by a wine. The term "aroma" is used to refer to the aromatic elements of a young wine, whilst the "bouquet" is the smell which results from ageing, storage and maturing and becomes noticeable over time.

There are three types of aromas in a wine:

PRIMARY AROMA. Each variety gives a wine its identity through its structure, its sugar level and its aromatic properties as a function of the intensity and the refinement of the perfume essences of its fruit. These aromas are fruity (i.e. they evoke the aroma of fruit) and floral (rose, geranium, etc.). The process of vinification must develop and foster the aroma of the fruit – the wine is more aromatic than the grape.

SECONDARY AROMA. This develops during the alcohol and malolactic fermentation stages. the yeast and bacteria produce secondary compounds which have an aromatic impact. On the other hand, as wine is a hydro-alcoholic solution it acts as a solvent for the volatile substances which are produced.

TERTIARY AROMA, OR BOUQUET. This is a combination of the previous two, to which are added the aromas from barrel ageing and those produced during the bottle ageing stage. The quality of the smell of the wines is principally governed by its primary aromas. Ageing begins with a loss of aroma in the new wine which has been weakened by carbon dioxide during fermentation and the subsequent operations to which it has been subjected. The bouquet is formed through two separate processes. The first involves contact with the air during barrel ageing which creates an oxidative bouquet with aromas of apples, nuts, wood tones, etc., and the other takes place during the ageing in bottle stage. The transformation of the primary aroma into the bouquet takes place as a result of various chemical reactions, leading to a more smooth and harmonic aroma, with complex and subtle nuances and a certain diminution in the fruity aromas.

TYPE OF AROMA	CLASSIFICATION OF SMELLS	EJEMPLOS
Primary	Floral	Rose, violet, geranium, magnolia, jasmin, lime blossom.
	Herbaceous	Green leaf, Straw, hay, tea, tobacco, bay leaf, coffee, mint, wood undergrowth.
	Fruity	Peach, apricot, apple, plum, cherry, cassis, quince, raisin, fig, orange, mango, pineapple.
Secondary	Etherous series	Yeast, ferment, acetaldehyde, honey, milk chocolate, banana nail varnish, yoghurt, lactic, dairy, butter.
Tertiary	Spices	Aniseed, mint, pepper, liquorice, clove, cinnamon, walnut, nut, vanilla, bay leaf, bitter almond.
	Balsamic and woody	Cedar, chestnut, sandalwood, pencil shaving, liquorice, oak.
	Chemical	Acetic acid, vinager, phenol, iodized, medicinal, alcohol, petrol, sulphurous, sulphydric, rubber.
	Empyreumatic	Toast, coffee, toasted almonds, cocoa, chocolate, caramel, pipe smoke, smoked, incense.
	Animal	Musk, game, hide or leather, hessian, stables, horse.

To evaluate a wine from an olfactory standpoint, it is important to quantify the aromatic intensity. To do this, each taster defines his or her own scale which can be summarised, in a very simplistic way, as follows: poor or weak, neutral, perfumed, aromatic, big bouquet, etc.

A qualitative evaluation of aroma is measured by refinement or quality, with complex and sophisticated aromas from aged wines being more highly rated than simple ones such as a fruity or floral aroma.

THE TASTE

Since the time of Aristotle, the contrast between sweet and unctuous, salty, sour, and sharp and bitter has been recognised. In 1914 Cohn defined the four basic taste sensitivities of the tongue:

SWEET. This is situated at the front of the tongue on the tip and is stimulated by sugar, alcohol and the glycerol produced in alcohol fermentation.

SALTY. This is registered on either side of the front of the tongue. A salty taste comes from the dissolved mineral salts in the wine.

SOUR. This is perceived at the sides of the tongue and underneath it. It is triggered by the acids in the wine, such as tartaric, malic, citric and lactic, etc.

Different types of decanters. Decanting allows the wine to be oxygenated which can be advisable with some bottles of a certain age but may also cause accelerated oxidation with very old bottles.

BITTER. The receptor cells are underneath and at the back of the tongue and are only triggered on swallowing. It is usually provoked by the polyphenols in the wine which come from the skins and pips of the grape.

These four tastes are complemented by a fifth, UMAMI, which corresponds to monosodium glutamate (msg), was propounded by the Japanese and is very common in Asian food (fish, soy sauce, etc). The SOUR taste is not a pure one. It comes from a mixture of bitter and acidic tastes. Sensitivity to the four basic tastes varies greatly from one person to another. Differences in the speed of perception are due to the fact that the different tastes are not all perceived in the same area of the tongue.

The SMOOTHNESS INDEX can be defined as the balance between sweet flavours and acid and bitter ones and could be represented by the following formula:

Smoothness index = alcohol content − (total acidity + tannins).

AREAS OF TASTE ON THE TONGUE

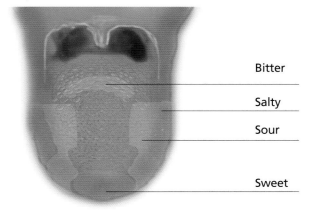

Bitter

Salty

Sour

Sweet

The mouth has exceptional chemical sensitivity which can be seen as a mucosal alarm response to attacks by certain molecules which is why different areas of the mouth perceive certain tactile and temperature sensations that are more related to the sense of touch than that of taste.

ASTRINGENCY is a sensation of dryness and roughness to which the buccal mucosa respond. The tongue does not move over the palate, gums, lips or teeth with its usual smooth movement, but instead seems to have become scratchy. This astringency is produced by the tannins in the wine and depends on their size (the medium sized are the most astringent), which is why during grape ripening, the vinification process and the subsequent ageing aims to achieve more polymerised tannins. There are various types of tannins: noble, flavourful tannins appear in the ripe fruit of top quality varieties and in grand and old bottles of wine; acid, sharp tannins appear in thin and aggressive wines; rough and very astringent tannins appear in young wines and press wines; maderized tannins come from oak barrels and, lastly, green tannins come from green grapes or from the wines of low quality wine-growing areas.

Another chemical sensitivity reaction is the CAUSTICITY, or burning, reaction which is produced by high concentrations of alcohol.

The PRICKLING sensation is more complex and is felt at the tip of the tongue when tasting recently fermented wines or sparkling wines and it is caused by the carbon dioxide. From a tactile perspective it is perceived as a series of light touches which cause a prickling feeling.

The mouth is also capable of perceiving KINAESTHETIC sensations which are involved in feeling a wine's texture, or body. In this respect, wines are described as light or slight, as with white wines, or big with a full structure when referring to more complete red wines.

Lastly, there is LENGTH which is the combination of taste, olfactory and tactile sensations. Length is not always pleasant (a wine which tastes of mold will have long and unpleasant length). Taste length is based on the acid and astringency sensations. In white wines, acidity dominates the end of the length and makes it possible to detect the final impressions of balance and freshness, or alternatively of hardness or greenness. In red wines it is the varied and complex tastes of the tannins which dominate the length.

TYPES OF TASTINGS

Tasting can be classified according to different aims. A tasting may be done to determine defects or virtues of a wine (possible diseases, bad taste or smells, defective vinification processes, bouquet, etc.); the geographic origin of a wine; the variety or varieties of grapes used; the approximate age of the wine; the type of ageing, if any, etc.

The most simple tasting is where two or more wines are offered in separate glasses and the tasters are asked whether they are different wines and, if so, which is the better. This is called blind tasting. A three-way test involves offering three glasses, two of which contain the same wine and the third a different one. This pushes the concept of the rigorousness of tasting to its limits. Another method which avoids too much subjectivity is to carry out the tasting with a team of tasters, trying to ensure that the group is as homogenous as possible. Each taster will act alone and make notes separate from the others, without seeing or hearing the other tasters' opinions.

TEMPERATURE

The temperature of a wine has a very significant effect on the olfactory and taste impressions, both qualitatively and quantitatively. Wines can only be compared if they are at the same temperature. Aromas and bouquets are exaggerated at temperatures above 18°C, reduced at 12°C and neutralised at 8°C.

TEMPERATURE	TYPE OR STYLE OF WINE
8°-10° C	Syrupy and aromatic
	Southern whites
	Dry northern whites
	Naturally sparkling
	Slightly sparkling
	Carbonated
	Rosés
	Dry liqueur wines
	Pedigree dry whites
10°-12° C	Naturally sweet wines
	Liqueur wines
	Young, light and fruity reds
15°-17° C	Aged reds (less than 6 years)
16°-19° C	Red Fine Wine:
	Reserva and Gran Reserva
	(aged more than 6 years)

The recommendation has always been that wine should be served at "room temperature" although a more correct way to express it would be to say that the wine should be served at "bodega temperature", i.e. about 15°C. The concept relates to the ambient temperature in the châteaux of France before central heating existed which would have been very different from the comfortable room temperatures that we know today. The table shows several recommendations regarding the temperature at which a wine is to be served and drunk.

Although we are accustomed to drinking white wines at between 8° and 10°C, in order to bring out their freshness and liveliness, certain wines such as the most recent Lagar de Cervera and other wines, display their varietal character and aromatic intensity better at 14°-15°C.

THE TASTER'S SURROUNDINGS

This is a very important factor and one which greatly influences the intrinsic subjectivity of the tasting. The ideal time is the later morning when the taster will feel hungry and his or her taste sensitivity will be heightened. Bodegas and laboratories are not good environments for tasting as the olfactory sense will not be able to achieve accurate results, either because of tiredness or deterioration (in a laboratory there may be an overly strong "cleaning smell" or one of alcohol distillation etc.).

Tasting can also be affected by adjustment phenomena or familiarity with a certain defect. If a wine with a certain defect is tasted regularly, the sensory organs become used to the defect and their perception threshold goes up. Furthermore, unpleasant tastes such as sharp, bitter and astringent ones tire the palate when it is exposed to them repeatedly.

Different glasses for tasting wine, eau-de-vie and champagne. Generally a wine tasting benefits when the glasses are of large capacity, made of crystal and have a wide mouth and large body. Champagne, on the other hand, requires a thinner and longer body in order to protect the bubbles.

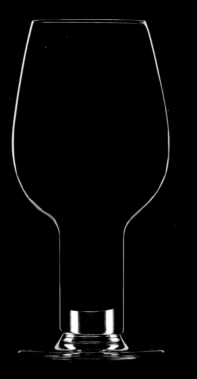

La Rioja Alta S.A.   **FICHA DE CATA**

NOMBRES Y APELLIDOS:

| MUESTRA N.º | | CATADOR N.º |

☐ Blanco   ☐ Tinto   ☐ Rosado   Fecha_____

1º EXAMEN VISUAL	**SUPERFICIE DEL LIQUIDO** brillante-sin brillo-límpido-matizado-trazas oleosas.		
	COLOR	**VINO BLANCO**	Claro con reflejos verdes o amarillos-amarillo pálido-dorado-amarillo pajizo-ámbar.
		VINO ROSADO	Pálido-con reflejos rosáceos o violetas-gris rosado claro-rosado oscuro ojo perdiz-piel de cebolla.
		VINO TINTO	Tinto con reflejos Vermellón o violaceo-rojo cereza-rubí-granate-oscuro-teja.
	ASPECTO		Cristalino-brillante-límpido-velado-turbio-apagado-plomizo-turbio con depósitos.
	BURBUJAS		Rápidas o lentas en formarse-inexistentes-pesadas-ligeras-grandes pequeñas.

CALIFICACION MAXIMA 4 puntos

2º EXAMEN OLFALTIVO	**PRIMERA IMPRESION**		Agradable-ordinario-desagradable.
	AROMA	**INTENSIDAD**	Intenso-suficiente-flojo inexistente.
		CUALIDAD	Muy fino peculiar-terruño-distinguido-fino-ordinario-poco agradable-grosero-desagradable-punzante.
		CARACTER	(Primario-secundario)-maderizado-rancio afrutado-floral-herbáceo-animal-ciruela-melocotón-manzana-grosellas-fresa-frambuesa-avellana-almendra-nuez-trufa-canela-miel-caramelo quemado-regaliz-tabaco-violeta-especias no determinadas-cedro-abeto-a polvo-vainilla.
		DURACION	Largo-mediano-corto.
	OLORES ANORMALES		Anhídrido carbónico-sulfuroso-mercaptano-descompuesto-madera-maloláctica-acético-moho-corcho.

CALIFICACION MAXIMA 4 puntos

EXAMEN GUSTATIVO	**SABORES Y SENSACIONES ORIGINALES**	**DULZOR** — **Azucar**	Licoroso-azucarado-dulce-seco-brut.
		Glicerina y Alcohol	Pastoso-untuoso aterciopelado-fluido.
		ACIDEZ — **Excesiva**	Acido-verde-mordiente-acidulo.
		Equilibrada	Fresco-vivo.
		Insuficiente	Plano-flujo.
		CUERPO — **Poder Alcoholico**	Generoso-vigoroso-cálido-pesado-suficiente-ligero.
		Constitución	Lleno-graso-redondo-pleno-ligero-delgado.
		Tanino	Rico y bueno-equilibrado y bueno-insuficiente-astringente-amargo.
		AROMA DE BOCA — **Intensidad**	Grande-mediana-débil-corto-largo.
		Cualidad	muy fino-elegante-agradable-común-pobre.
		Naturaleza	Floral-afrutado-herbáceo-complejo-joven.
	SABOR ADQUIRIDO O ACCIDENTAL	**TERRUÑO**	Acusado-sensible-agradable-desagradable.
		ENFERMEDADES	Grasa-agriado-agridulce-quebrado-gusto azufre-rancio-picado láctico-picado acético.
		ACCIDENTES	Gusto pútrico-a moho-a lías-a madera-a corcho-a metal-a sulfídrico (huevos podridos)-herbáceo-acre.
		EQUILIBRIO	Armonioso-amplio-correcto-angañoso-anguloso-fatigado.
		POSTGUSTO	Recto-franco-desagradable-estable-inestable.
		PERSISTENCIA	Muy largo-largo-mediano-corto.
	Conformidad a la Denominación, genuinidad o al tipo:		

CALIFICACION MAXIMA 9 puntos

CONCLUSIONES	**Interpretación de la Cata** Carácter del Vino-su futuro-consejos eventuales. FIRMA CALIDAD DE CONJUNTO, MAXIMO 3 puntos. PUNTUACION TOTAL _____

⌇ An example of a very detailed tasting card, of the style used in La Rioja Alta, S.A., in around 1950.

It is important to stress just what a significant role subjectivity plays in wine tasting. Tasting is greatly influenced by the current state of mind of the taster. There are times when it might be said of a bottle that "It is not the same as yesterday". Although this may in fact be true, it is also perhaps more often the case that what is not the same as yesterday is the taster. One's frame of mind and circumstances on a given day at a given moment greatly influence perception during tasting which, without us realising it, is conditioned by the tangible circumstances of the moment. At times and perhaps erroneously. a defect may be detected in or a virtue attributed to a wine which in reality it does not have.

GLASSES FOR TASTING

The first drinking vessels were a form of ladle made of clay, wood, ceramic or even metal in a dome-like shape. In the 15th century small, flat cups with smooth or thick sides were called "winetasters", now known by the Burgundian name of "tastevins". The tastevins; these were made of silver, were 29 mm deep and held 9 centilitres. The Burgundian tastevins were decorated with a combination of clusters and tendrils. Seen from the side, the wine appeared lighter in colour, thinner and more translucent.

The Bordeaux cup owes its heritage to the ancient Greek and Roman cups. Smooth and free of decoration, this silver cup held 7 centilitres and had a convex bottom which allowed the brilliance of the bottom to be seen through the liquid. However, these tastevins presented a significant disadvantage in terms of loss of aroma and were difficult to taste from, as a result of which glasses for drinking and tasting were subsequently developed.

For a professional taster, the glass is the tool of his trade. Crystal tasting glasses date back to the 17th century, until which point the most commonly used tasting vessel was the chalice. In the mid 19th century, balloon shaped crystal glasses were introduced and these are the forbearers of the tasting glasses used today.

The nature of the glass, its form and volume influence the perception of sensations just as much as the way in which the wine is served. Wines of a certain quality need to be served in a glass with a stem, made of clear, uncoloured crystal, with smooth walls and with no decoration. In 1970, at the peak of the Denominaciones de Origen, the tasting glass was standardised. Other, more innovative designs have since been developed, which are specifically for certain types of wine. Some manufacturers have produced outstanding designs which are adapted to each region and variety.

The cleanliness of the glasses is of paramount importance and optimum results in this regard are achieved by washing them with a cloth, without reusing them, in hot water with no detergent and then leaving them to drain upside down. There is no need to dry the glasses and they should be kept in odour-free glass cabinets. Before serving a wine it is advisable to rinse the glass with the same wine which is to be tasted so as to eliminate any adverse smells.

TASTING METHODOLOGY

Tasting a wine requires a methodology which can ensure reliability in the organoleptic analysis. The first step is to observe a wine's colour and its tonality, by tilting the glass at a 45° angle so that the depth and chromatic intensity can be observed by looking at the glass from above. Ideally, this should be done against a white background, such as a sheet of paper, so that the tones of the wine stand out as much as possible.

The wine is initially sniffed without moving the glass; thereafter the wine is swirled round the glass as this encourages the release of the volatile components. The upper part of the glass is then brought up to the nose at an angle of 45°, in order to maximise the exposed surface area of the wine and thereby achieve a greater sensory impact. On smelling the wine, the first thing to check is whether it is a clean wine; the next step is to try to detect the smells which are emerging, evaluating them for intensity and attempting to store them in the memory so that they can be noted later.

A large sip of wine is then taken and held and swirled round the mouth. The lips are then half-opened while the wine is still in the mouth and a little air is taken in which helps release the volatile elements. While the wine is in the mouth, the taste sensations are evaluated and the wine's balance and length assessed. After five to eight seconds, the wine can either be swallowed or, in the case of professional tasters, spat out. At that point, attention is focussed on the aftertaste, i.e. the combination of sensations remaining in the mouth and nose after the wine is swallowed, concentrating particularly on its intensity and length, which is very long in the case of great wines.

Julio Sáenz, our Technical Director demonstrates the steps in tasting: decant, pour the wine, observe the colour, analyse the aroma, taste the wine, savour the aftertaste.

ANALYSIS OF THE WINE

Historically it was considered advisable before tasting to carry out certain routine analyses to determine the chemical characteristic of the wine which will influence its sensory properties. There are many parameters to be verified, but the main ones are: total acidity, volatile acidity, true acidity or pH, sulphur anhydride or SO_2 in the wine, density, reductant sugars, ethyl alcohol or alcohol content, organic acids (malic, lactic and tartaric), dry extract and, lastly, colour indices.

These are the most common routine analyses carried out in a bodega. Advances in technical instrumentation have enabled installation of new equipment in our laboratories which provide a great deal of information about the wines and enable evaluation of a greater number of compounds in the wine. Chromatographs have enabled quantification of compounds which are present in tiny amounts, in the order of nanograms per litre. Lastly, analyses are done of metals (iron, copper) cations (potassium, sodium), anions (sulphates, chlorides), aromatic compounds, residues of phytosanitary products, compounds responsible for bad smells in the wine (TCA, phenols), etc.

In addition to the physico-chemical tests, microbiological analyses are done (yeast and bacteria counts) for fermentation monitoring and to ensure the stability and wellbeing of the wine and musts. Multi-parameter analysers such as the FOSS WineScan® are the most recent additions to the wine-making industry's equipment. They use infrared technology to determine various parameters and provide a large amount of data in a short time. All the analysis methods are approved by the OIV (International Organisation of Vine and Wine) which acts as a reference in the publication of official analysis reports.

The Casa-Palacio at Torre de Oña, S.A. is a good example of the concept of "Living the Wine". Here, in the beautiful surroundings in the heart of the San Martin estate, visitors can enjoy both the vineyard and the bodega.

THE GREAT WORLD OF WINE

The Casa-Palacio at Aster is a perfect example of the chateau or estate winery style, in this case in Ribera del Duero.

he great world of wine has become a universe to be explored, discovered and enjoyed over many years. It is going through enormous changes which have transformed it into one of the most dynamic sectors in the Spanish economy. Wine tourism is growing rapidly and makes it possible not only to drink the wine but also to experience living the wine.

LIVING THE WINE

It is fascinating to consider the long road that this thousand-year-old activity has travelled over the course of history. But it is also wise to look at the changes which have taken place over recent years and which deserve to be described as impressive, at the very least. This "miracle of transformation" has enabled wine to go from being a necessary but incidental component of parties and meals to having top billing at any type of celebration. An intense passion for wine and all its trappings has transformed it into a fashionable product which people talk about, express opinions, reflect and explore, all of which has bestowed on wine a seductive glamour and created limitless interest which is two-fold in nature.

The first aspect has been the influx into the wine sector of people with interests in other economic sectors, as diverse as the fashion industry, construction, information technology and art. These people have focussed both their attention and their savings on investment in bodegas, either as partners or indeed as sole proprietors. This was the starting point for many of the new bodegas which sprang up across the length and breadth of Spain during the 1980s and 1990s and it is a phenomenon which was, of course, repeated in other wine-growing areas of the world. It must be remembered that, for example, some of the most illustrious wineries in the renowned Napa Valley in California were founded by successful IT entrepreneurs from Silicon Valley, brokers and financiers, artists and cinema producers, etc.

Nevertheless, the vast majority of mere mortals obviously cannot afford the luxury of owning their own bodega, a fact which has led to the second aspect, namely the huge interest in visiting and enjoying bodegas owned by others. All of these factors taken together have led to the emergence of a novel and significant concept: living the wine. Bodegas are no longer simply places where wine is produced.

249

Bodega Lagar de Fornelos, S.A. (Rías Baixas). The dining room, known as the "Club de Cosecheros", at La Rioja Alta, S.A. (Haro).

Nowadays, people want to get to know them personally, to discover as with La Rioja Alta, S.A. their centuries old history, to understand the production and ageing processes, etc. But people also want to move among the barrels and vineyards, to enjoy and relax in the buildings, to relish eating in the dining rooms or tasting wines in the bodega and, more and more, to get to know the people – the oenologist, the owners, etc. All of these many activities combined are known as "enoturismo", or wine tourism, an expression which has still, however, not been recognised in the Diccionario de la Real Academia de la Lengua Española (Dictionary of the Royal Academy of the Spanish Language) but which, through repeated use and the force of custom, will doubtless be included eventually.

There can, however, be no doubt that visiting wine-producing areas is today a marvellous and very different form of tourism. Furthermore, and regardless of the traveller's

TODAY IT IS NOT ENOUGH JUST TO DRINK A WINE – IT MUST ALSO BE LIVED, BY VISITING THE GROWERS AND THEIR HOMES, WALKING AMONG THE VINES……

level of passion for wine, there are aspects which are a siren call in their own right. This is true of, for example, the exhilarating, diverse and stunning landscapes in which a great many bodegas and vineyards are located.

And how can one begin to describe the extraordinary architectural developments instigated by many entrepreneurs in recent years in their new bodega premises, commissioning and committing to iconoclastic buildings designed by internationally renowned architects? Moreover, some of the bodega reception areas and shops can compete with the grandest boutiques in the heart of some of the world's biggest capitals. And it almost goes without saying that the quality of the wine is fundamental and is the entire raison d'être for a bodega although it must not be forgotten that promoting the image of a wine and its background can contribute enormously to the prestige of the wine itself. All bodegas are, therefore, delighted to welcome visitors each and every day.

It is clear that there has been a vast and still ongoing reshaping of what is on offer to the wine tourist. Some bodegas have magnificent spas to relax in and reap the therapeutic benefits of the different constituents of the wine. Other bodegas offer bicycle or riding tours around the vineyards, trips in hot air balloons, trips by train across the region, wedding receptions with a gastronomy/wine focus, etc. Many businesses are conscious of the undoubted success and upsurge in the popularity of wine and all its trappings and have decided to specialise in this field, forming management companies for activities and services relating to wine. Likewise, public institutions and organisations located in the various Denominaciones de Origen have not be slow in turning wine into one of the main attractions when designing cultural programmes, offering tourist packages, scheduling routes or organising a wide variety of other events, with the aim of harnessing the massive interest which the world of wine is currently generating.

This spectacular growth in the "wine phenomenon" has benefited enormously from the mind-boggling exchange of information resulting from the widespread use of the Internet which provides, in real time, all sorts of information about innovations at bodegas all over the world, their latest launches and, of course, everything about the wine tourist experience that they offer. These virtual journeys also enable opinions to be shared about the wine industry and have contributed to a tremendous global and cultural gain. There are thousands of specialised sites, forums and blogs about wine on the Internet, a new conduit with unimaginable potential. La Rioja Alta, S.A., of course has a website (www.riojalta.com) which contains not only all the information about our wines and bodegas but also an electronic copy in English and Spanish of the very book that you are holding.

Although there are many variants and ideas contained within this new concept of the oenological universe, we are facing it with optimism and passion based on our perfectionism and profound conviction in the cultural value of wine, its links to a place and its history. We strive every day and have done so since we were founded to produce top quality wine. However, today we also work tirelessly to go beyond the wine, to strengthen its cultural value and to take care of and share the magnificent heritage of our bodegas.

Every day friends and clients come with many and varied aims to our delightful and attractive premises. At present, a visit to any one of our four bodegas can encompass many activities: learning about our century old history, seeing and enjoying the magical process of making wines, learning about tasting, fine dining in our charming private dining rooms, relaxing in our Casa-Palacios... all under the spell of the beauty, tradition and elegance which enhance each visit.

Our exceptional surroundings are also enjoyed by all those companies that choose to swap their everyday working environment for that of our bodegas which can offer the perfect alternative for meetings, seminars, conferences, presentations, press conferences, brainstorms, board meetings, etc. All our bodegas offer spacious and multi-purpose function rooms which are equipped with state-of-the art multimedia facilities, to guarantee the success of all kinds of business meetings and all of this in remarkable surroundings, far from the madding crowd and in an ambience of absolute discretion, elegance and calm. To this end we have, for example, refurbished and specially adapted the Ermita de Santiago del Siglo XVII, which is just metres from our Torre de Oña, S.A, bodega at Páganos (Álava).

The previous page shows images from various bodegas, such as the boutique designed by the architect Zaha Hadid at the Bodega R. López de Heredia in Haro (La Rioja); the Museo de la Cultura del Vino de la Fundación Dinastía Vivanco at Briones (La Rioja) [Museum of Wine Culture, Vivanco Foundation]; the shop at the Bodegas Muga in Haro (La Rioja) designed by the architect Iñaki Aspiazu; the Bodega Señorío de Arinzano de Julian Chivite at Aberín (Navarra) by the architect Rafael Moneo; the Bodega Codorniú in Sant Sadurní d'Anoia (Barcelona), the work of the architect Josep Puig i Cadafalch, the gardens created by the landscape gardener Luis Vallejo at the Bodega Vega-Sicilia in Valbuena del Duero (Valladolid), the "City of Wine" at the Bodega Marqués de Riscal by the architect Frank O. Gehry in Elciego (Álava); the Bodegas Terras Gauda, a fine example of the small single wine estate at O Rosal (Pontevedra).

Staircase at Áster.
This Casa-Palacio is
available for the use of
our friends and clients.

If one looks in greater detail at the current noticeable change of focus in respect of wine and its multi-faceted culture, it is clear that the relationship between the client and the bodega has over several decades become increasingly close and more personal and is now carefully nurtured and fostered.

One obvious example of this significant and direct relationship between the bodega and the consumer is the exclusive wine clubs which are established in their own names, in our case the Club de Cosecheros.

In 1976 La Rioja Alta, S.A. instituted a pioneering initiative in Spain which was born out of precisely this concern to foster and enrich a cordial relationship, which we were among the first to understand, needed to go much further than just the buying and selling of high quality wine.

In order to understand the philosophy behind this, we must look to the past and board that "old train" which, at the end of the 19th century and due to the phylloxera plague, brought French wine merchants to the lands of Rioja to sample and select the different wines and later "reserve" (this is the origin of the term "Reserva") one or more consignments of barrels which would then remain in the bodega until ageing was complete, before travelling to French territory.

THROUGH THE CLUB DE COSECHEROS, WE WOULD LIKE TO SHARE EVERYTHING THAT WE HAVE AND EVERYTHING THAT WE KNOW

As time passed, the buyer began slowly to have confidence in certain firms and started to leave the choice of wines to the discretion of his wine suppliers. Despite the gradual arrival of bottling and the rise of modern commercial practices, certain clients still relied on this custom to request the privilege of a place or a barrel in "their Bodega". La Rioja Alta, S.A., was happy to satisfy these very personal requests by devising a system which would enable a large number of friends and regular consumers of our wines to have greater access to these "reserves".

This mutual trust can be summarised on the one hand as being the member's confidence in the bodega, by buying in advance a barrel of wine which is as yet unborn and, on the other hand, the overwhelming responsibility which the bodega assumes from that moment on towards this loyal member: the choosing of certain plots of land for the vines, the best harvests, a batch of wine which is exclusive and not openly available on the market, and which will respect to the greatest possible extent all the characteristics and idiosyncrasies of its place of origin.

In short, it is a very big wine which can carry such promise, responsibility, dedication and friendship. These are the essential values which we wanted to bring to the Club de Cosecheros at Torre de Oña, S.A., which was formed in 1997, and to the Club de Cosecheros at Áster, founded in 2002. Almost 35 years later, we continue to plan each offering for our three Clubs with the same vision and sense of responsibility which we are very proud to assume.

Everything that is served in our private dining rooms has been made in-house by our own cooks. The photograph shows the kitchens at Torre de Oña.

Moreover, belonging to one of our three Clubs entitles members to certain exclusive privileges, amongst which we would highlight the opportunity to have personalised bottle labels, to enjoy our premises, to take part in tasting courses or to have priority reservations for our private dining rooms. Furthermore, our members have access to our complete oenological and gastronomy collection, are offered special prices for our wines and other products, receive up-to-date information about the most recent innovations at our bodegas, as well as our quarterly Information Newsletter and can, as one of many privileges, reserve the suites at our bodegas, at Torre de Oña and Áster, to enjoy unforgettable days as guests in our Casa-Palacios.

We are able thus to establish a worthwhile relationship with wine consumers and enthusiasts, which we continue to foster. The Club de Cosecheros is an act of openness and trust in our clients and friends and we are able, therefore, to guarantee a totally personalised and top quality service at all of our establishments. There is absolutely no doubt that our Clubs personify the very considerable ability that La Rioja Alta, S.A., has to adapt perfectly to this new concept of "living the wine".

The universe of wine is, in short, an art, a culture, an environment, a and a way of life which is transformed into a unique experience which can satisfy both the tangible desires of the senses and the more ephemeral longings of the spirit.

Dining room at Áster, where we can offer a splendid meal overlooking the rows of French oak barrels.

Detailing at our premises – warm, decorative and beautifully presented.

259

Dining room at Torre de Oña, S.A. Both this residence and that at Áster are available to our clients and friends.

RIOJA HARVESTS SINCE 1890

Vendimia de 1892.
Uva ingresada.

El dia 4 Octubre   10.932
"   "   5   "   34.317
"   "   6   "   44.850
"   "   7   "   57.398
"   "   8   "   76.219
"   "   9   "   67.314
"   "   10   "   52.853
"   "   11   "   47.835
"   "   12   "   49.798
"   "   13   "   33.166
"   "   14   "   28.214
"   "   15   "   29.341
"   "   16   "   23.109
"   "   17   "   32.245 3.245
"   "   18   "   37.761
"   "   19   "   23.000
"   "   20   "   17.117
"   "   21   "   12.906
"   "   22   "   5.352
                        ‾‾‾‾‾‾‾
                        683627

Record of grapes delivered to the bodega when La Rioja Alta, S.A. was a mere two years old (1892).

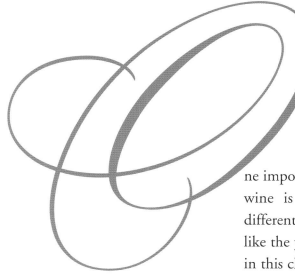ne important element of the beauty and mystery of the world of wine is the qualitative and quantitative disparity between different harvests. Have you ever wondered what the vintage was like the year you were born? We will try to satisfy your curiosity in this chapter.

RIOJA HARVESTS SINCE 1890

In marginal or peripheral climatic areas such as Rioja or Ribera del Duero, quality can attain a level of very refined characteristics, with exquisite wines being produced from time to time. However, the marginal climate is problematic and unpredictable and may cause extreme variations in the wines. As an example, an area such as Haro, heart of the Oja river valley and thus the hub of the Rioja region, produces wines with an average alcohol content of 12°, but in 1972 it was 7° and in 1981 it was 14.5°.

From time to time the climate conditions conspire to give very rounded musts with high levels of colour, fixed acidity and alcohol content, which forecast wines of excellent quality. These are the great vintages, the "millesime" as the French would put it. Quantity, quality and climate are inextricably linked in a complex way but there are pointers of interest.

It is accepted that the vegetative cycle requires a succession of days with an average temperature above 10°C. Ordinarily in Rioja this would be the case between 1st April and 15th October, which constitutes about 195 days. The higher the number of days, the greater the likelihood of wines of an excellent quality.

The most important conclusions are:

1. Better quality assumes rationed quantities of grapes, although in some harvests which have been classified as excellent, quantity and quality have coincided. Examples of this latter contention are the harvests of 1964, 1985, 1989, 1995, 2004 and 2005.
2. There is no consistency in the cycle of excellent harvests. It can be said that the popular concept of "global warming" does seem to be coming true and that we are about to enter an period in which vegetative cycles will grow longer, which presupposes better quality. Between 1970 and

Part of our history: when mules provided the pulling power and, below, a collection of antique bottles ranging from 1890 to 1964.

1980 it was difficult to achieve excellent harvests, whilst since 1980 the quality has been high and it is difficult to find a bad harvest. Although 1984 was not ideal, it was nowhere near as deficient as the previous decade.

3. From the 2001 harvest onwards, there has been a noticeable and significant increase in the mean alcohol level and somewhat of a drop in the acidity. The Rioja Alta region has traditionally produced great wines with an alcohol content of 12.5° but is now consistently producing wines of 13.5° or even 14°. The consequences of this change are not yet clear but both oenologists and wine producers are devoting a great deal of energy to researching it.

A summary of data about the Denominación de Origen Calificada Rioja produced principally by Don Manuel Ruiz Hernández. (The classification of the harvest shown is the official one from the Regulatory Body and may not be the same as the internal classification of La Rioja Alta, S.A. The production volumes refer to certified litres).

1890	VERY GOOD	
1891	MEDIOCRE	
1892	GOOD	
1893	VERY GOOD	Very low yield.
1894	EXCELLENT	
1895	VERY GOOD	Good ripening except for Garnacho.
1896	DEFICIENT	Green wines, because of insufficient ripening. Rioja Alavesa can be considered GOOD.
1897	EXCELLENT	In general wines with very good colour.
1898	EXCELLENT	Perfect ripening in Rioja Alavesa.
1899	VERY GOOD	Wines with high fixed acidity.
1900	REGULAR	Poor ripening.
1901	VERY GOOD	Balanced wines.
1902	VERY GOOD	Moderate alcohol content and low fixed acidity.
1903	GOOD	Low yield.
1904	VERY GOOD	Very balanced wines. High alcohol content in Haro.
1905	VERY GOOD	Low yield.
1906	EXCELLENT	Very good balance between high alcohol content and acidity. Flea beetle attack on the vines.
1907	VERY GOOD	Violent storm in Haro in July. High alcohol content.
1908	MEDIOCRE	Yield generally very low. Hail storm in August. Wines with low alcohol content. Rioja Alavesa GOOD. Frosts in April.
1909	GOOD	Very low Tempranillo yield per hectare. Attacks of mildew and oidium. Frosts in May and wet August.
1910	MEDIOCRE	Very deficient ripening. Severe frosts in April. August very wet.
1911	MEDIOCRE	Attack of mildew in August. Snow in April. Hailstorm in Haro on 8th June. Hot, wet summer. 194 day cycle.

1912	DEFICIENT	Deficient ripening. Cold spring, not below freezing. Dry summer and rainy September.
1913	GOOD	Poor acidity in Tempranillo. Low yield. Heavy frosts in April. Dry July.
1914	MEDIOCRE	Very bad flower fertilisation. Few grapes and poor ripening. Very dry summer.
1915	MEDIOCRE	Mildew attack. Rioja Alavesa VERY GOOD quality. Dry summer and rain only in September.
1916	MEDIOCRE	Poor Tempranillo ripening. 220 day cycle. Abnormal leaf growth in April. Dry summer, cool September and hot autumn.
1917	GOOD	
1918	GOOD	
1919	VERY GOOD	Very good ripening.
1920	EXCELLENT	Wines with high alcohol content and intense colour.
1921	GOOD	Bad oidium attack. Strong easterly winds.
1922	EXCELLENT	Very balanced wines. High yield.
1923	MEDIOCRE	In the area specifically around Haro, GOOD.
1924	EXCELLENT	High yield per hectare.
1925	VERY GOOD	High yield per hectare.
1926	DEFICIENT	Tempranillo, however, excellent in Haro. Very low yield.
1927	DEFICIENT	Severe mildew attack.
1928	VERY GOOD	210 day cycle. Prevailing northerly and easterly winds. Frosts during harvest. Tempranillo with very low acidity.
1929	MEDIOCRE	Uneven wines, some very good. Excellent Tempranillo ripening. High yield.
1930	DEFICIENT	Deficient ripening. High yield.
1931	VERY GOOD	Wines with high alcohol content. Above 15° in some areas.
1932	MEDIOCRE	Low alcohol content. Mildew attack.
1933	MEDIOCRE	Very uneven wines, with moderate alcohol content. Low yield.
1934	EXCELLENT	Alcohol content not particularly high but very well-balanced wines. Very high yield per hectare.
1935	VERY GOOD	Very well-structured wines with high alcohol content.
1936	MEDIOCRE	Very low alcohol content. Mildew attack. Low yields.
1937	MEDIOCRE	Low alcohol content. Severe drought. High yield.
1938	DEFICIENT	Uneven harvest. In some areas very good wine.
1939	MEDIOCRE	High yield per hectare. 190 day cycle. Moderate alcohol content. Mildew attack.

1940	MEDIOCRE	Low yield. Mildew attack.
1941	GOOD	Moderate yield. Annual rainfall of 530 l/m². Frosts in spring.
1942	VERY GOOD	210 day cycle. Annual rainfall of 476 l/m². Wet summer. Wines with high alcohol content and strong colour.
1943	GOOD	High yield. Annual rainfall of 410 l/m². Wet summer.
1944	GOOD	215 day cycle. July and September cold, August hot. Little rain, but well distributed.
1945	DEFICIENT	205 day cycle. Frosts in May and very cool August. Little rain, poorly distributed.
1946	MEDIOCRE	205 day cycle. Cold summer. Rainfall badly distributed, very heavy in April.
1947	VERY GOOD	210 vegetative cycle. Hot summer and very low annual rainfall. Severe drought during cycle.
1948	EXCELLENT	205 day cycle. Previous winter warm. Some frost during spring. Little rain but, significantly, 25 l/m² fell during August. Cool summer.
1949	VERY GOOD	205 day cycle. May very cold. Hot summer. Heavy rainfall in August and September triggered mildew attack.
1950	MEDIOCRE	200 day cycle. Frosts in April, September cold, poor ripening. June very rainy.
1951	MEDIOCRE	215 day cycle. Previous winter warm. Frosts in April and severe mildew attack.
1952	EXCELLENT	212 day cycle. July cool. August very hot. Well distributed rainfall but August dry.
1953	DEFICIENT	205 day cycle. Severe frosts in April. June cold. Very hot summer.
1954	GOOD	205 day cycle. Frosts in April. Prevailing westerly winds. Cool summer.
1955	EXCELLENT	195 day cycle. Frosts in April. Rainfall well distributed throughout cycle.
1956	GOOD	175 day vegetative cycle. Previous winter very cold and frosts in spring.
1957	MEDIOCRE	210 day vegetative cycle. Previous winter extremely cold and dry. June very rainy.
1958	EXCELLENT	188 day vegetative cycle. Prevailing westerly winds. Moderate annual rainfall of 410 l/m², very well distributed with 100 l/m² falling during the summer, which was very beneficial.
1959	VERY GOOD	200 day vegetative cycle. Frosts during the spring, June cold. Rainfall widely distributed during vegetative cycle, although low during budding and plentiful in September.
1960	GOOD	Volume of wine 133 million litres. 180 day vegetative cycle, cut short by spring frosts. Very dry year. Heavy rain during harvesting. Strong winds from the south.
1961	GOOD	Harvest produced 71 million litres of wine. 207 day cycle. Strong influence of southerly winds on ripening, September hot and wet. Mild autumn.

After the harvest, the vineyard
is transformed by all the
striking colours into a stunning
landscape at our Labastida bodega,
built in 1996.

1962	VERY GOOD	Volume of 124 million litres. Previous winter very wet but not particularly cold. No spring frosts. Summer hot and moderately wet.
1963	MEDIOCRE	Volume of 104 million litres. 190 day vegetative cycle. Severe spring frosts. Grapes in good condition but unripe before fermentation. Previous winter cold. Frosts in April in Haro.
1964	EXCELLENT	For some, the best vintage of the century. Volume of 135 million litres against an average for 1960-1970 of 100 million litres. Excellent and plentiful. 210 day vegetative cycle, June relatively cold and one day of frost in April. Prevailing westerly and northerly winds. Annual rainfall 460 l/m² and, although sparse, there was rainfall in July and August.
1965	DEFICIENT	Volume of 109 million litres. 190 day vegetative cycle. Previous winter very cold. Severe drought, prevailing westerly winds. Between May and August rainfall of only 38 l/m².
1966	MEDIOCRE	Volume of 98 million litres. February warm, frosts in March. May and July unusually cold. 200 day vegetative cycle. Prevailing westerly winds and mildew attack.
1967	MEDIOCRE	Volume of 94 million litres. 205 day vegetative cycle. Severe spring frosts in March and April which badly affected Rioja Alta and Alavesa. Very dry year for vines, rain arriving after the harvest. Hot summer.
1968	VERY GOOD	Volume of 89 million litres. 210 day vegetative cycle. April cold. August quite cold. Cool summer.
1969	MEDIOCRE	Volume of 85 million litres. 205 day vegetative cycle. Heavy rainfall in spring and September. Prevailing northerly winds.
1970	VERY GOOD	Volume of 113 million litres. 195 day vegetative cycle. Previous winter cold and wet. Late budding. No spring frosts. Hot and wet summer. Hail in June. Autumn mild with very late leaf fall.
1971	BAD	Volume of 55 million litres. 202 day vegetative cycle. Previous winter very cold and very dry. Spring very wet. Frosts in May. Mildew attacks. Summer and ripening period very dry. Mild October.
1972	BAD	Volume of 98 million litres. 192 day vegetative cycle. Late budding in very cold weather. Summer cold. Severe mildew attack.
1973	GOOD	In our opinion VERY GOOD. Volume of 128 million litres. 180 day vegetative cycle. Previous winter cold and dry. No spring frosts. Our cold weather station did not record any appreciable rainfall. Very irregular rainfall during cycle. Hot summer.
1974	GOOD	Volume of 130 million litres. Very short vegetative cycle, only 170 days. Previous winter very cold and with rainfall of 130 l/m². Heavy rain at the beginning of spring. No frosts. Hot and dry summer.

1975	VERY GOOD	Volume of 84 million litres. 185 day vegetative cycle. Previous winter very dry (60 l/m²). Late budding. Wet spring. Hot summer and very hot weather during harvest.
1976	GOOD	Volume of 93 million litres. 180 day vegetative cycle. Previous winter cold and dry (only 90 l/m²). March very cold. Late budding. Hot and wet summer. Difficult ripening and uneven quality depending on area.
1977	MEDIOCRE	Volume of 66 million litres. 200 day vegetative cycle. Adverse conditions for vines. Frosts in spring were not severe but were persistent and were followed by very heavy rainfall and a cold summer, although a mild autumn.
1978	VERY GOOD	Volume of 78 million litres. 193 day vegetative cycle. Previous winter cold and somewhat damp (130 l/m²). Severe frosts in April ruined 20 days of vegetation. Summer and autumn dry. Wines from this vintage are, some years later, EXCELLENT.
1979	MEDIOCRE	Volume of 140 million litres. 210 day vegetative cycle. Previous winter mild and wet. No spring frosts. Expectation of good quality wine right up to August because of good weather. Prevailing winds then changed to southerly and easterly. Heavy rainfall during ripening led to wines of unstable colour.
1980	GOOD	Volume of 141 million litres. 192 day vegetative cycle. No spring frosts. Cool and wet summer. Ripening in moderate temperatures. Wine with moderate colour but little body.
1981	VERY GOOD	We disagree with the official classification and consider this vintage EXCELLENT. Volume of 135 million litres. 228 day vegetative cycle. Previous winter cold and with rainfall of 130 l/m². Frosts in April, initially with cold winds and then snow. First half of June hot, latter half cold. Until that point, poor conditions for quality but a hot autumn compensated.
1982	EXCELLENT	Volume of 125 million litres. 210 day vegetative cycle. Previous winter mild (115 l/m²). Budding in hot weather. First week of July very hot. Moderate rainfall in July and August (18 l/m²) and September (40 l/m²).
1983	GOOD	Generally good wines. Volume of 108 million litres. 216 day vegetative cycle. Previous winter cold, with 150 l/m². Light frost in spring. Hail in May in the Najera, Cenicero and Lapuebla areas. Abnormally heavy rainfall in August (190 l/m²). At the end of September morning dew damaged leaves in Abalos, Baños, Elciego and Lapuebla. Harvest carried out in hot weather. Wines with strong colour.
1984	MEDIOCRE	Deficient wines in certain areas. Volume of 107 million litres. 210 day vegetative cycle. Previous winter mild and wet. Frost on 13th May in Rioja Alta and Alavesa. Hail on 4th September in Villalba, Briñas and Labastida. Considerable loss on 4th October caused by Hurricane Hortensia. Late harvest. Cool fermentation. Sound wines of little colour.

Reception and shop of La Rioja Alta, S.A. (Haro), where we welcome all our visitors.

1985	GOOD	Unusual harvest. Volume of 170 million litres and 188 day vegetative cycle. A weak harvest was expected and the volume was unprecedented. Very good wine in high areas and late harvest. Difficult fermentation because of accumulation of grapes. EXCELLENT quality in Rioja Alta.
1986	GOOD	Volume of 120 million litres. 195 day vegetative cycle. Heavy frosts in April and summer was dry but not hot. Annual rainfall was only 255 l/m^2, compared with an average of 450 l/m^2.
1987	VERY GOOD	Volume of 133 million litres. 200 day vegetative cycle. Light frost in May. Previous winter typically cold and summer warm – a very continental climate. Summer both warm and dry and annual rainfall only 286 l/m^2, as against normal rainfall of 450 l/m^2.
1988	GOOD	Volume of 131 million litres. 198 day vegetative cycle. Previous winter mild. Excessive rainfall in spring and early summer. Annual rainfall 795 l/m^2, leading to mildew although the Rioja region successfully kept it at bay. Cool summer. Very maritime climate.
1989	GOOD	Volume of 164 million litres. Erratic ripening – very rapid until the beginning of September and then slower. Viura ripened early whereas Tempranillo ripened late. Variable and tricky fermentation in some bodegas. Carbonic maceration reacted very well in the Villalba/San Vicente/Samaniego area. The Garnacho in Rioja Baja was surprisingly good on ripening, exceeding 16° alcohol content. Reds are of a similar quality to 1985, i.e. EXCELLENT.
1990	GOOD	The barrel wine can now be classified as VERY GOOD. Volume of 161 million litres. 195 day vegetative cycle. Very dry year with total rainfall of 365 l/m^2, against an average of 450 l/m^2. A vintage which is renowned for its body and smoothness.
1991	VERY GOOD	Volume of 145 million litres. Sporadic mite attacks. Irregular rainfall. Late ripening in some areas, with rain interfering with the harvest, leading to unstable colour.
1992	GOOD	Total volume of 150 million litres. 212 day vegetative cycle. Very high annual rainfall of 673 l/m^2, at the wrong times: heavy during flowering caused setting failure, or non-fertilisation, in Tempranillo. Heavy rain also during the harvest, from 12th October onwards. Grapes picked before this produced EXCELLENT wines, whilst those picked later produced DEFICIENT wines of light and unstable colour.
1993	GOOD	Volume of 174 million litres. Dry, frost-free spring. Summer damp with normal average temperatures, but at unusual times. August was hotter than July, although generally the reverse is true. September cold, with rain during the first 10 days. The rain was needed but arrived too late in Rioja Baja although it was beneficial in Rioja Alta.

1994	EXCELLENT	Volume of 169 million litres. 195 day vegetative cycle. Hot and dry summer. From veraison onwards grapes ripened very quickly, if somewhat unevenly, with sugar and acidity being ahead of colour. Very healthy grapes. Early fermentations were rapid, resulting in occasional high temperatures. Later fermentations were slow, so results were inconsistent. Ultimately the balance between alcohol content, acidity and colour was very good.
1995	EXCELLENT	Volume of 218 million litres. The weather in September favoured high quality because early ripening in the first few days of the month was followed by a cold spell and 13 days of well distributed rain. October was dry and unusually hot, in fact hotter than September, leading to a high level of ripening. Generally the wines had a high alcohol content. At times the turbulent fermentation was slow whilst the slow fermentation was turbulent.
1996	VERY GOOD	Volume of 244 million litres. The vegetative cycle took place in superb conditions. The weather in September was not auspicious and led to uneven ripening. Alcohol content and colour of wines appropriate for the characteristics of the vintage.
1997	GOOD	Volume of 254 million litres. The vegetative phase of the vine was early compared to previous years. Budding was very good. The summer was excessively rainy and the ripening was therefore very uneven. The characteristics of the wine are within the parameters for its quality.
1998	VERY GOOD	Volume of 274 million litres. The vegetative cycle took place in superb conditions, which led to anticipation of superb quality. However, rainfall in September brought forward the harvest and slowed ripening. The harvested grapes were generally healthy, with moderate alcohol content and colour intensity in those wines from early harvest grapes and a higher quality in those from the later harvest grapes.
1999	GOOD	Volume of 216 million litres. Spring frosts led to a poorer harvest than anticipated. The most notable consequence was a huge jump in the price of the grapes (record prices to date in the history of Rioja). The harvested grapes were of acceptable quality (correct alcohol content and high polyphenol content).
2000	GOOD	Volume of 311 million litres. Record harvest which produced wines of variable quality. A high percentage of the wines was classified as EXCELLENT for ageing, above all in those vineyards with limited production and grapes from old vines.
2001	EXCELLENT	Volume of 242 million litres. Harvest considered historic on the basis of its virtues, with alcohol content, colour and acidity all above the average for all harvests. Wines of great homogeneity, ideal for long ageing.

2002	GOOD	Volume of 197 million litres. Harvest very varied, with some wines having very good structure and perfect for ageing, others will not meet expectations.
2003	GOOD	Volume of 298 million litres. Notable for very high temperatures during summer, producing over-ripe wines with low acidity.
2004	EXCELLENT	Volume of 270 million litres. Harvest very well suited to long ageing due to correct alcohol content, good concentration of colour agents and good aromas.
2005	EXCELLENT	Volume of 274 million litres. Excellent vintage, similar to 2001. The absence of botrytis across the whole of the Denominación is worthy of note. The wines produced are very well suited to long barrel ageing, with a balanced concentration of phenol compounds.
2006	VERY GOOD	Volume of 278 million litres. Very varied harvest, with a significant imbalance between glucometric and phenolic ripening, particularly marked in vineyards with overly loaded stocks. More moderate loads have yielded wines which will support moderate ageing.
2007	VERY GOOD	Volume of 274 million litres. Very good quality harvest for wines intended for moderate and long ageing, with good weather conditions in the final phase of ripening. Wines with good colour layer, considerable varietal aromatic intensity and good balance between alcohol content and final acidity. The Regulatory Body made the classification criteria more strict for this harvest (it would have been EXCELLENT) and future ones.
2008	VERY GOOD	Volume of 272 million litres. Heavy rainfall during vegetative cycle and at the end of October delayed harvesting of the grape. The harvest was done on a very selective basis. The resulting wines have a lower alcohol content compared to previous years, but a better balance in terms of acidity. Very aromatic and balanced wines, typical of the upper region of La Rioja. High quality harvest in our Group.